SPEAKING ILL OF THE DEAD

Jerks in Washington, D.C., History

Emilee Hines

Guilford, Connecticut

I dedicate this book to my editor, Erin Turner,
who suggested that I write it,
and to my friends and family who think it's
going to be a big seller.

To buy books in quantity for corporate use
or incentives, call **(800) 962–0973**
or e-mail **premiums@GlobePequot.com.**

Copyright © 2011 by Morris Book Publishing, LLC

Text design by Sheryl P. Kober
Project editor: Kristen Mellitt
Layout artist: Kevin Mak

Library of Congress Cataloging-in-Publication Data is available on file.

ISBN 978-0-7627-6033-6

Printed in the United States of America

10 9 8 7 6 5 4 3 2 1

The evil that men do lives after them. The good is oft interred with their bones.

—Marc Antony, *Julius Caesar* by William Shakespeare

Acknowledgments

I especially thank Jerry Liedl, who solves my computer problems, gets pictures into the right format for publishing, and helps me in many other ways.

I thank the staff of the Henderson County Library for procuring the many hard-to-find books I needed for research; my critique partners Dorothy Staffieri and Elaine Trull for patiently reading and improving my writing; Bruce Franklin, who critiqued my chapters on Mitchell Palmer and Joseph McCarthy and revealed that his mother once double-dated with McCarthy. (She said "he was a blowhard even then.")

I also wish to thank Paul Hogroian, Jason Bowling, Sandy Angle, Gretchen Batra, Shirley Blackwell, Becky and Ernest Bowling, Sarah Bowling, Betty Freund, Kerry and Marianne Hines, Margaret Hines, Bill Holmes, Shirley Liess, Leslie Newell, Anne Sternad, and Elizabeth Scott.

Contents

Introduction

We are often admonished not to speak ill of the dead, as they are no longer around to defend themselves, but that is just what the series *Speaking Ill of the Dead* does.

We need and appreciate good people to keep civilization functioning, yet we enjoy speaking ill of the bad ones. Outrageous behavior grabs our attention, and bad news makes the headlines. Good news and competence we take for granted. A biographer of General Robert E. Lee said it was difficult to write an interesting biography of Lee, as the Virginian never did anything bad.

I had no such problem in researching and writing about the "jerks" in this book.

We all know a few jerks. They do or say something stupid or thoughtless that makes us want to avoid them. We may even have been jerks ourselves occasionally, doing or saying something we regret.

Jerks in power reach a higher level of stupid, thoughtless behavior. Their words and actions can have consequences for millions of people. Washington, D.C., is the seat of power, not just for America, but for the world, and thus provided fertile territory to locate jerks suitable for *Speaking Ill of the Dead: Jerks in Washington, D.C., History*. And because the words and deeds of famous political figures have been well documented, my research was made easier than if I had chosen obscure jerks.

There is a saying, "Power corrupts and absolute power corrupts absolutely." As incumbent politicians now seem to have year-round, lifelong tenure, they have much more power and hence more scope for sin. They also have access to the money that helps pay for their transgressions and for the lawyers who often rescue them from punishment.

Many of the jerks in this book transcend mere jerkiness. They are guilty of adultery, assault, blackmail, bribery, deception, extortion, slander, and even murder.

Earlier, their crimes and misdemeanors could be hidden, often with the help of a friendly press, so that Thomas Jefferson could instigate action against an enemy but add, "Keep my name out of it." Sometimes the truth about transgressions emerged only after the death of the guilty one. We were taught in American history of the good they did, and almost all of the jerks did some good as well as bad, but we didn't know about the bad.

That hero-worshipping attitude has changed. Now we know. Ever since Joseph McCarthy's bullying was exposed by TV coverage, we have watched, appalled at what those in power are doing. With the widespread use of cell phones that take and transmit photos, no one is safe from scrutiny, powerful or not. We have learned that we must "respect the office if not the officeholder."

There was such a broad array of jerks to choose from in writing *Speaking Ill of the Dead: Jerks in Washington, D.C., History* that I could not include them all. The fact that all perpetrators had to be dead eliminated many of my favorite possibilities, and the cutoff time, in the 1950s, eliminated others.

I chose those I consider the most egregious, who did something corrupt, despicable, or criminal. There are many "second-string" jerks who did nothing when they should have acted: Presidents Van Buren, Fillmore, Pierce, and Buchanan, for example. The late nineteenth century had its own share of forgettable presidents, but America was not as important a nation, and their activities thus went relatively unnoticed.

I eliminated John Adams even after researching his career and writing a 3,500-word chapter. He wasn't "jerky" enough. He was competent and intelligent, but he was vain and jealous of George Washington, writing that the first president was popular because he was tall, handsome, and from Virginia.

Henry Clay might have qualified. He always wanted to be president, and he twice passed up a chance to run as vice president, considering it a "dead end" and thus beneath him. Both times the president died in office and Clay's ambition would have been fulfilled. Bad choice, Henry. John Calhoun was a jerk for leaving behind his young wife and firstborn child only a week after the baby's birth, to go to Washington. These two plus Daniel Webster—who borrowed money and never repaid it—were guilty of pushing President James Madison into declaring the War of 1812 and for decades controlled the Senate and its members.

Benjamin Butler, so brutal that the South referred to him as "the Beast," deserves a place for many reasons: He was an incompetent general who made up for it with ugliness, especially in New Orleans. He hanged a man for pulling down the U.S. flag, he ruled that any woman who insulted a Union soldier would be treated as a prostitute, and he was accused of stealing silver spoons from Southern homes. About all he did as a congressman was lead in the impeachment of Andrew Johnson. Butler must also be credited with launching the career of another jerk, Dan Sickles. I would have included Butler, but there were so many other jerks in the antebellum and postbellum period, and I tried to cover the entire history of Washington, D.C., from its beginning to the 1950s.

The jerks in this book are all men. I'm not being sexist in my choices. Women just didn't have the access to power that would have qualified them as real jerks compared with those I have chosen. The few who came close paid a high price. Mary Surratt was hanged for her part in President Lincoln's assassination. Emma Goldman was deported for preaching anarchy. Mary Lincoln was a jerk for her jealousy and extravagance, which sometimes took her husband's mind off weighty matters of national importance, especially the Civil War. However, Mrs. Lincoln did not profit from her behavior as most jerks did, and she didn't plan and scheme. She was later committed to a mental institution and died a lonely, sad woman.

Woodrow Wilson was a jerk for several reasons, but especially for the divisions he made of empires on the losing side in World War I. His mistakes are still with us, as the nations he helped create were and are unstable, and instability leads to dictatorships and other wars. Wilson deserves a book all his own.

Alexander Hamilton and Matthew Lyon had to be eliminated because their jerky deeds were performed while the nation's capital was first in New York and then in Philadelphia, and as the title of this book states, the setting must be Washington, D.C.

But there were plenty of others to include.

Marc Antony said in Shakespeare's *Julius Caesar*, "The evil that men do lives after them. The good is oft interred with their bones. So let it be with Caesar."

And so let it be with the "jerks in Washington, D.C., history." May you enjoy reading about the evil that lives after these men as much as I did in researching and writing about them.

Almost an idol to some, Thomas Jefferson hid dark secrets.

CHAPTER ONE

Thomas Jefferson:
Hero or Hypocrite?

Who dares criticize Thomas Jefferson? He's an American icon, a Founding Father, honored every July Fourth as the author of the Declaration of Independence. Innumerable sites are named for him, and his image is one of four carved on the stone face of Mount Rushmore.

Yet beneath the fame and adulation, he was at base a jerk, vindictive and petty, managing to appear "above it all" while blaming others when things went wrong. He bore grudges and often accused others of the very underhanded deals he himself had made. Some biographers are reexamining Jefferson, as long-lost letters and documents come to light and DNA evidence makes a strong case for what was once thought of only as a scandalous rumor.

Jefferson was a Virginia aristocrat, related to many of the political leaders and landed gentry of the colony. He graduated from the College of William and Mary, studied law, and was elected to the Virginia House of Burgesses. He acquired land and built Monticello, his mountaintop home near Charlottesville, with slave labor.

In 1772 Jefferson married the rich, young widow Martha Wayles Skelton, who inherited 11,000 acres of land and over a hundred slaves. One of these slaves was her mulatto half-sister Sally Hemings, who came to live at Monticello.

Within the next ten years, Martha had seven pregnancies. Only three daughters survived. Then Martha died. Jefferson was half-mad with grief, but he eventually returned to public life and was sent by the American government to be ambassador to France.

Jefferson deserves praise for many accomplishments. He managed to get a loan from the Dutch for the fledgling American government at a critical time. He went against his own idea of what was constitutional in buying the vast Louisiana Territory, doubling the size of the United States; and his scientific curiosity led him to send Meriwether Lewis and William Clark to explore the new territory. Instead of paying tribute to the Barbary pirates of North Africa who had threatened American and European shipping and had taken American prisoners, he sent the American Navy and Marines to fight—and won. He established the University of Virginia, the first secular public university in America.

However, his accomplishments were accompanied by his contempt for George Washington, John Adams, and Aaron Burr, and his hatred for his cousin John Marshall, fellow Cabinet member Alexander Hamilton, the British, and all Federalists. He often worked through other people, pretending to be above politics, claiming he was just a simple farmer who wanted domesticity at Monticello. Some contemporaries said Jefferson could compartmentalize his thinking, so that he actually believed that what he was saying and doing at the moment was the true and right thing. Others saw him as a hypocrite.

The hypocrisy began with the Declaration of Independence, which is full of exaggerations and inaccuracies. Jefferson referred to King George III as a tyrant, guilty of heinous crimes, when in fact the king was one of the most mild-mannered of European rulers. If Jefferson had actually known George, the two might have liked each other, for they both enjoyed tinkering and inventing mechanical devices.

The lofty sentence, "We hold these truths to be self-evident, that all men are created equal, that they are endowed by their Creator with certain unalienable rights, that among these are life, liberty and the pursuit of happiness" was Jefferson at his most hypocritical. On a day-to-day basis, he didn't follow any of it.

He never thought that women or blacks or Indians were his equal or, for that matter, that white men who disagreed with him were his equals, either. He thought that his design for America's future was the right one and that whatever he had to do to see it happen was acceptable. However, if it involved chicanery, his involvement should be kept secret. He wrote letters after the fact "reminding" his followers that they had acted of their own volition.

Jefferson owned slaves his entire life. He took Sally, then eleven, and her brother James to Paris, where James learned the French language and cooking. The slaves could have been freed then, as France didn't recognize slavery. Jefferson's solution, which he advised another American to do, was simply not to report the slaves to French customs. Sally was seventeen and possibly pregnant when she returned from Paris. She was only one-fourth black, and her children, even lighter, passed as white. The only slaves Jefferson freed were Sally's siblings and children, but not Sally herself. When an inventory was taken of his estate after his death in 1826, Sally—the probable mother of his children—was listed with a value of $50!

Jefferson believed the other slaves were better off in bondage to him than they would be freed. He designed Monticello so that the slave quarters were not visible from the main house; thus, visitors would not be reminded of slavery. He stated that if slaves were freed, it must be done all at once and they must be resettled in a separate state or country, as they could never live peacefully alongside whites. He considered Indians as savages who also could not live peacefully with whites. He thought all Indians should be moved west of the Mississippi.

Both Alexander Hamilton and Aaron Burr wanted to free America's slaves. They earned their living as lawyers in New York and hired servants to do their work, while slaves made up a substantial part of Jefferson's wealth. Most of his wealth came from land ownership, and the land couldn't be farmed without slave labor. This difference of opinion caused the first division among the three men.

During the Revolutionary War, Burr, Hamilton, John Marshall, and, of course, George Washington all joined the military, and though Burr resigned after a few years, he had a successful stint in the army and acted bravely. The others fought on until victory came at Yorktown in 1781. Jefferson didn't fight for independence, nor did he explain why he never went to war. He wrote and spoke of the need for a "bloody revolution" every twenty years—but it would have to be fought by someone else, not him.

In 1779 Jefferson was elected governor of Virginia. Governors then served one-year terms but could be repeatedly reelected. Jefferson, lacking military experience, was a poor choice to be a wartime governor. Virginia's economy was a shambles, and he was not the leader to set things right. He didn't get along with the legislature and approved sending Virginia troops to be part of a strike on Detroit just when his state was endangered. Traitor Benedict Arnold led British troops up the James River to Richmond. On the way, he laid waste to Jefferson's Tidewater property, stealing or killing livestock, destroying crops and buildings, and burning the capitol at Richmond. A contemporary critic, Henry "Lighthorse Harry" Lee, in his history of the Revolution, pointed out that if Jefferson had given instructions for dispersing Virginia's important documents and her staple crop, tobacco, much would have been spared. Instead, the tobacco was all in warehouses in Richmond and the documents were left in the capitol, making their destruction simple.

Jefferson and the legislature moved to Charlottesville and were pursued by British troops. Jefferson narrowly escaped capture, and he was later criticized for fleeing rather than fighting. He had resigned as governor two days before the attempted capture, stating that the job needed someone with military experience. That someone was Thomas Nelson, who at Yorktown even shelled his own house, which was being used as headquarters for General Charles Cornwallis.

After the American victory at Yorktown, the new nation struggled along for several years under the loose governance of the Articles of Confederation. It soon became obvious that a stronger union was needed, and a Constitution was written, setting up three branches of government, with a strong executive, the president. George Washington was elected president, and John Adams, returned from diplomatic duty, became vice president. The capital was New York.

On Jefferson's return from France, Washington asked him to be secretary of state. It was then a multitask job, involving domestic as well as foreign matters. He accepted but was never comfortable in the administration. He opposed Secretary of the Treasury Alexander Hamilton's financial program to establish the credit of the new government. The program entailed paying wartime debts to foreign countries, redeeming at face value the bonds that people had purchased to support the war, having the central government take on the states' debts, and establishing a national bank and a tax system. Jefferson himself was in debt to British merchants and wanted to repudiate them. In addition, Virginia had paid off its state debt, and he objected to Virginians being taxed to pay for other states' debts.

The gap between Jefferson and Hamilton widened at the time of the French Revolution. Jefferson rejoiced when French citizens seized the Bastille in 1789 and overthrew the monarchy, seeing it as a revolution similar to America's. He continued his support of the French movement even when the king and queen were beheaded and bloodshed became common in France. Hamilton was aghast and urged President Washington to cancel any alliances with the French, maintaining—correctly—that we had dealt with the monarchy, not the group that had assumed power.

Washington managed to achieve a compromise between Hamilton and Jefferson: In ten years, the nation's capital would be moved to its present location, adjoining Virginia, in return for which Jefferson would persuade Virginians to vote in favor of Hamilton's financial program. Jefferson did, but he still distrusted Hamilton.

Jefferson hired Philip Freneau, editor of *The National Gazette*, as a translator in the State Department, mainly as a means of support for the journalist. Freneau published screeds against Hamilton, including letters written anonymously by Jefferson himself, accusing Hamilton of treason in aiding the British. When the nation's capital was temporarily moved to Philadelphia while the new Federal City was being built, Jefferson saw to it that Freneau came along and refused President Washington's request to fire him.

Jefferson also acted as a jerk in the matter of Edmond Genet. The French government had sent Genet to instigate rebellions in Louisiana and Spanish Florida, in order to seize those territories from Spain and return them to France. He landed at Charleston, South Carolina, home of many French émigrés, where he was entertained royally. Eventually he made a triumphal journey to the national capital. Genet carried a commission for General George Rogers Clark, hero of the American Revolution, making Clark a major general in the army of the French Republic. As such, Clark was to organize and lead an army to attack and seize New Orleans.

Genet revealed all his plans to Jefferson. President Washington had expressly forbidden any Cabinet officers from cooperating with Genet or anyone else attempting an invasion of a nation with which the United States was at peace. Instead of reporting the plot to the president, Jefferson sent a botanist west with Genet's message to George Rogers Clark, who was expected to assist Genet. Genet meanwhile outfitted a ship in direct opposition to President Washington's orders, attacked and seized a British ship, and brought it into Delaware waters. The United States had to pay the British for the loss of this ship. Washington ordered Genet deported to France. Knowing that he would be guillotined if he returned, Genet instead settled on Long Island and married the daughter of Governor George Clinton, who was to become Jefferson's vice president.

Both Jefferson and Genet escaped any punishment for what would essentially have been treason had the plan succeeded. Later Jefferson was to charge Burr for essentially the same actions that Jefferson had been complicit in with Genet.

When Washington retired at the end of his second term as president, Jefferson thought his time had come to hold the highest office. At that time, candidates did not run on "tickets," but singly.

Electors cast votes for two candidates; the man receiving the highest number became president, the second most, vice president, even if they were from opposing political parties. John Adams, the Federalist, was elected president; Jefferson, the Republican (later to be called Democratic Republican and later still, Democrat) became vice president.

The two men disagreed on nearly every issue. Jefferson, when working with Adams on the Declaration of Independence, or consulting him about diplomatic matters abroad, had referred to Adams as his leader and mentor. Now he turned his scandal-mongering journalists on President Adams. The leading one was James Callender, who for years had criticized Jefferson's opponents, publishing scurrilous, often untrue, stories about them. With Jefferson's financial and editorial support, Callender published a pamphlet called *The Prospect Before Us*, in which he referred to Adams as—among other terms—a "corrupt and despotic monarch." When Adams protested, Jefferson denied having anything to do with the attacks, but Callender had saved Jefferson's letters commending *Prospect* as "producing the desired effect." Adams cut off communication with Jefferson. Callender was fined and jailed under the terms of the Sedition Act, which made it a crime to criticize the government.

Burr first supported Jefferson for president, but then decided that he would run for president himself. When Burr and Jefferson tied for president in 1800, the election was to be decided by the House of Representatives, as the Constitution specifies. Jefferson, through intermediaries, made a deal with Federalists, agreeing among other things not to remove Federalists from appointed offices. A few votes were switched on the thirty-sixth ballot in the House of Representatives, making Jefferson president. He then accused Burr of the very bargaining attempt he himself had made. Jefferson soon had impeachment proceedings brought against leading Federalist judges, released Callender and others imprisoned under the Sedition Act, and refused to appoint to public office any candidates recommended by Vice President Burr.

Callender asked for the job of postmaster of Richmond, Virginia, and when Jefferson failed to appoint him, Callender turned on the president. "I made you president by lying," he shouted outside the President's House (now the White House), "and I can unmake you by telling the truth." He proceeded to publish accusations that Jefferson had tried to seduce the wife of a neighbor, that he had paid a debt with depreciated money—both of which Jefferson admitted—and that he was the father of Sally Hemings's children. Jefferson never denied the last charge, only saying that "every decent man is revolted by this filth." Apologists for Jefferson have said that his nephews were responsible for Sally's pregnancies, but one otherwise adoring biographer, Dumas Malone, charted Jefferson's whereabouts and concluded that he was at Monticello nine months before each birth.

Jefferson wrote to Adams, attempting to reestablish communication. He again claimed he'd had nothing to do with Callender's attacks on Adams but complained that Adams had acted incorrectly by appointing Federalist judges the night before his term ended. Abigail Adams read the letter and wrote to Jefferson that he was either a hypocrite or delusional and added a "serves you right" note about Callender's latest articles: "The serpent you cherished . . . bit the hand that nourished him." It was eight years before the two former friends, Adams and Jefferson, wrote to each other again.

Meanwhile, Callender got a job writing for a Richmond newspaper and soon became one of the editors. Then one summer morning in 1803, Callender's body was found floating in two feet of water in the James River. A coroner's report indicated that the journalist had drowned while drunk. Jefferson must have been relieved at the scandalmonger's death. Rumors circulated at the time that his death might not have been accidental.

Jefferson, the Republican, had a Republican-dominated House of Representatives and a Senate that was evenly divided between Federalists and Republicans, but the Judiciary was totally Federalist, having been appointed by Washington and Adams. In the waning hours of his presidency, Adams had filled all the remaining judicial positions with Federalist appointees. This was a barrier to Jefferson's clean sweep of the government. Jefferson proposed that only Congress should be the judge of whether its acts were constitutional, which would have been absurd. He also wanted the president to have the power to remove judges as he wished, but according to the Constitution, judges were appointed for life. He feared that they could undo what he had done as president, so he determined to repeal the Judiciary Act of 1801, which had increased the number of judges, and to remove other judges by impeachment.

When the Judiciary Act was brought up for repeal, the vote in the Senate was a tie. Burr broke the tie, voting for repeal. The following year, in the case of *Marbury v. Madison*, Chief Justice John Marshall ruled that the act was unconstitutional anyway, but he also established the right of the Supreme Court to interpret the constitutionality of acts of Congress. This was a setback for Jefferson, but only a temporary one. He next had Justice Samuel Chase impeached, ostensibly for his behavior in certain cases, but basically because he was a Federalist and had upheld the Sedition Act. The impeachment failed.

Despite Burr's support in repealing the Judiciary Act, Jefferson had determined to get rid of his ambitious vice president. Burr begged to have another term, but Jefferson chose the aged George Clinton, who would be no threat to Jefferson's plan for a Virginia dynasty of presidents.

Burr left Washington and made several trips west. It's unclear just what he intended. He did approach the British representative for support in taking Florida and Mexico from Spain. Could Burr have carried out his scheme? Whatever the truth, Jefferson accused his former colleague of treason. In a letter to Governor William Claiborne of Louisiana, Jefferson essentially advised him to "fudge" the law in dealing with Burr.

Enter William Eaton. This soldier of fortune had been consul of Tripoli and had led the overthrow of the corrupt ruler in Tripoli. He was back in Washington seeking reimbursement for his expenses and was being ignored by the government. Burr contacted him to be a possible military leader of an expedition against New Orleans, but gave no details.

Eaton told President Jefferson varying stories of the conspiracy, tailoring his story to what he thought the president wanted to hear. Suddenly a $10,000 pension was awarded to Eaton, and troops were sent to find and arrest Burr. At Burr's trial for treason in Richmond, Virginia, Jefferson directed the prosecution and attended the sessions. Eaton's testimony was vague, and no overt acts of treason had been committed. To Jefferson's chagrin, Burr was acquitted.

During Jefferson's second term, Britain and France—at war with each other—both attacked American shipping to keep supplies from reaching the other. Jefferson's solution was the Embargo Act, stopping trade with all nations. Only coastal trade was allowed. Jefferson was sure England could not do without our products and would soon agree to stop attacking our ships and impressing our men into the navy, but he misjudged. American farmers, manufacturers, and ship owners suffered, and the country plunged into a depression. War was postponed until Jefferson left office and his successor, James Madison, had to deal with it.

Back at Monticello, Jefferson had another chance to live up to the words of the Declaration of Independence. A young neighbor, Edward Coles, asked Jefferson to join him in freeing his slaves. The law required that freed slaves must leave the state within a year, but if several slave owners, and especially Jefferson, were to take a stand, the law might be overturned. Jefferson declined. Coles took his slaves to Ohio to free them and buy land for each, while the author of the phrase, "life, liberty and the pursuit of happiness," continued to own and exploit human beings.

In his declining years Jefferson designed the University of Virginia and persuaded the Virginia legislature to fund it, though it repeatedly overran his cost estimates.

Jefferson had no ability to manage money. He lived lavishly, buying horses, expensive wines, and vast numbers of books, but his biggest money mistakes were his constant rebuilding of Monticello and his building of a retreat, Poplar Forest, his vacation home ninety miles from Monticello. Before he died on July 4, 1826, he had sold off hundreds of acres and his library. His heirs had to sell his slaves and Monticello, but still faced a mountain of debt.

The outcome might have been different if he had paid more heed to his property and livelihood instead of attempting to destroy his political rivals.

SOURCES

So much has been written about Thomas Jefferson that research was almost overwhelming. He is one of the most written about of all Americans, and in addition to books about him, he is a major player in the biographies of his contemporaries.

For general histories of the period, I read the following: Marcus Cunliffe's *The Nation Takes Shape 1789–1837* (Chicago: University of Chicago Press, 1959); Marshall Smelser's *The Democratic Republic 1801–1815* (New York: Harper & Row, 1968); and Gore Vidal's *Inventing a Nation* (New Haven, Conn.: Yale University Press, 2003).

Biographies of Jefferson I read include these: Roger Bruns's *Thomas Jefferson* (New York: Chelsea House Publishers, 1986); *American Sphinx* by Joseph L. Ellis (New York: Alfred A. Knopf, 1997); Thomas J. Fleming's *Thomas Jefferson* (New York: Grosset & Dunlap, 1969); *Burr, Hamilton and Jefferson* by Roger G. Kennedy (New York: Oxford University Press, 2000); Dumas Malone's *Jefferson and His Time*, Volume 4, *Jefferson the President, First Term 1801–1805* (New York: Little, Brown and Company, 1970); and Joseph Wheelan's *Jefferson's Vendetta* (New York: Carroll & Graf Publishers, 2005).

Jefferson's rivalry with Alexander Hamilton was depicted in two volumes by Robert A. Hendrickson: *Hamilton II 1789–1804* (New York: Mason/Charter Books, 1976) and *The Rise and Fall of Alexander Hamilton* (New York: Van Nostrand Reinhold Company, 1981). Jefferson's attempts to control the judiciary are described in two biographies of his cousin, Supreme Court Justice John Marshall: Albert J. Beveridge's *The Life of John Marshall,* Vol. III, *Conflict and Construction* (Boston: Houghton Mifflin, 1919) and Bill Severn's *John Marshall, the Man Who Made the Court Supreme* (New York: David McKay Company, 1969).

The election of 1800 is ably covered in Edward J. Larson's eminently readable *A Magnificent Catastrophe: The Tumultuous Election of 1800* (New York: Simon & Schuster, 2007).

Virginia Cavalcade devoted the Autumn 1979 issue (Vol. XXIX, No. 2) to Thomas Jefferson. I read three of the articles: "The Hemings Family at Monticello," James A. Bear Jr.; "The Monticello Scandals," Virginius Dabney and Jon Kukla; and "James Thomson Callender," Charles A. Jellison. In other issues of *Virginia Cavalcade,* I read Elizabeth Langhorne's "Edward Coles, Thomas Jefferson and the Rights of Man" (Vol. XXIII, No. 1, Summer 1973) and "A Battle of Memoirs—Lighthorse Harry Lee and Thomas Jefferson," Charles Royster (Vol. XXXI, No. 2, Autumn 1981).

CHAPTER TWO

Timothy Pickering:
Once a Jerk, Always a Jerk

Some jerks blunder along, not realizing they are harming others, and some commit one huge, outrageous act, such as murder, that brands them forever. Timothy Pickering was of a third sort: He felt *his* way was always right no matter what his superiors—including two presidents of the United States—might want done. When things didn't go his way, he deliberately set out to get revenge. He shifted sides so often that no one knew for sure where his loyalties lay, but he managed to repeatedly talk his way into advantageous positions. Once in the job, he scorned those who had helped him get there.

He came by his attitudes honestly. His father, Timothy Pickering Sr. turned his back on his church over a minor disagreement and held to his Tory beliefs all his life, even though it meant being estranged from his son.

Young Timothy was sent to Harvard, which he hated. After graduation he studied law, and returned to Salem, Massachusetts.

He joined the exclusive Library Society in 1765, when he was twenty. The group was Loyalist, and this allegiance got Pickering a commission as a lieutenant of the local militia, a job he was totally unsuited for.

After British troops occupied Boston and the "Boston Massacre" occurred, Pickering broke with the Tories. Criticized as a turncoat, he responded that he was loyal to England but opposed to the policies of the king's ministers. This habit of playing both sides continued throughout his life.

The Pickering family was prominent, and his sisters had married influential men in Massachusetts. Because of this, Timothy was chosen a town selectman of Salem despite his wavering

Engraved by T.B.Welch from a drawing by J.B.Longacre after G.Stuart

TIMOTHY PICKERING.

Despite his sly appearance, two presidents trusted Timothy Pickering,
and he betrayed them both.
LIBRARY OF CONGRESS

loyalties. Then, even though he had opposed forming a Committee of Correspondence to keep the colonies apprised of each others' activities, the committee was formed and he was elected its chairman.

To punish Boston, Governor Thomas Gage moved the capital of the colony briefly to Salem and issued orders for the arrest of the Committee of Correspondence. Pickering was arrested, posted bail, and was released, leaving four of his committee members in jail. Gage's troops had a standoff with the town militia. The governor returned to Boston and revoked the charter for Massachusetts. Conflict between Britain and the colonies was heading toward war.

Pickering published a manual on the purpose and training of militia and was put in charge of the patriot militia. But he didn't want to fight; he just wanted the honor. He argued against doing anything in retaliation after the Battle of Lexington in April 1775. When the regular army organized to lay siege to Boston, Pickering argued for negotiations and refused to fight. Though some of his men enlisted, he took the others and returned to Salem.

Tories fled to Halifax, Nova Scotia, or to England, leaving many jobs to be filled by patriots. Thus Pickering was able to become both register of deeds and town clerk. He wanted to be justice of the court, but his refusal to join the army worked against him. He wrote an article saying that he didn't oppose fighting for political reasons but because he thought Massachusetts was unprepared for war. He got the justice job, as well as that of judge for three adjoining counties.

War came despite negotiations, and George Washington, commanding the Continental Army, suffered a series of defeats. Pickering reminded his friends of his assessment that the colonies were unprepared. Washington called for militia to fill the ranks of his men, who were leaving when their short-term enlistments ended. This time Pickering, as leader of the Essex Regiment, took his men to join Washington, whom he both admired and criticized.

Washington asked Pickering to head up the War Board, as adjutant general. Pickering liked the title but deplored the laxness and immorality he saw all around him. He said that the colonies did not deserve to win their independence but probably would because the British were worse. He saw his fellow New Englanders profiteering from selling food, clothing, forage for animals, wagons, and other goods needed for the army, and he criticized Nathanael Greene, quartermaster general, for putting up with theft among his employees. Greene's attitude was "do what you have to in wartime."

The situation was so bad that General Benjamin Lincoln was forced to surrender six thousand troops in South Carolina because he could not get supplies or transport for reinforcements.

A congressional committee investigated military procurement and called for it to be reorganized. The quartermaster was to be paid a salary rather than a commission on purchases, and the states were to provide a set amount of supplies. Pickering, who had complained of the corruption, was urged to take the quartermaster post. He didn't want it, but was caught. He would be responsible for all the logistics of the army: tents, hospitals, transport animals, lead for bullets, even the digging of latrines, as well as providing uniforms, weapons, and food. He was supposed to stay with the army and supervise the various activities but instead spent his time doing office work in Philadelphia.

The army's money situation grew desperate. Vendors wouldn't accept government certificates, fearing the government wouldn't redeem them. Pickering wanted to use the army to force citizens to provide animals and wagons, but Washington opposed the idea.

The situation was saved by Robert Morris, the richest merchant in America, who pledged his fortune to finance the war.

Even after Washington's victory at Yorktown made it clear the war was won and no more military procurement was needed, Pickering stayed on in his post. Congress in 1780 had offered a half-pension for life to those who stayed in the army for the duration of the war, and Pickering wanted to be sure he got the benefit. Both sides ceased fighting in April 1783, and later that year a treaty was signed.

In May 1783 Pickering and a friend set up a mercantile business, but economic bad times brought failure to them and many others. Pickering then planned to get rich by speculating in land in Pennsylvania and buying up soldiers' notes at a discount. He lost money on both enterprises, and his government job was finally eliminated in 1785.

Always overconfident as to what he could accomplish, Pickering next went to northeastern Pennsylvania, where he owned land in the Wyoming Valley. Overlapping land claims there had led to civil war. Pickering was convinced he could make peace between the groups and set up a functioning local government. He got himself appointed to all the county offices in the newly formed Luzerne County, but peace wasn't as easy as he had thought. The Pennsylvania legislature failed to settle the claims as he had expected, and when one of the troublemakers was arrested and taken to face trial, a group of rowdies kidnapped Pickering. They kept him on the move for nineteen days, during which he wrote to his wife, indicating that he did not expect to be ransomed and giving her instructions for running their farm since he might be away for a long time. Meanwhile, townspeople searched for him, and the kidnapping group broke up. He was released unharmed but had changed his mind about settling the land in Pennsylvania.

Despite Pickering's poor performance during the Revolutionary War, George Washington appointed him envoy to the Seneca Indians, with the promise of a regular government job when he returned.

This period of Pickering's life shows him at his best. He saw the good side of the Indians. They had been defrauded of their land, not illegally but unethically. There was no way to reverse the sales and get back their land, but he tried to make sure they didn't lose any more. He urged them to give up hunting and go into farming. The Indian chief Cornplanter agreed and drew up a plan for acculturating his people. They would need schools, farm tools, sawmills, and gristmills. Pickering agreed, and the plan was accepted by the government.

Before Pickering could get his promised government appointment, however, four Seneca were murdered near Fort Pitt. The Indians retaliated by killing nine people. General Henry Knox, secretary of war, reinforced the western forts. War with the Indians seemed inevitable.

Pickering got the Senecas' promise of peace and neutrality. President Washington was pleased with the neutrality treaty and named Pickering postmaster general.

In this job he was swamped by paperwork but unwilling to delegate any authority to others. He never grasped the concept of being an executive. Again, like the quartermaster post, this job required a lot of hands-on supervision. Pickering was responsible for post roads, hiring post riders, tracking down mail thieves, awarding mail contracts, and preparing legislation for the government.

He was dissatisfied with the postmaster job and was sent again as Washington's representative to the Indians. Without telling Pickering, Washington and Knox decided to forget acculturation for the moment and instead get several of the Six Nations to intercede with the hostile Ohio Indians.

The Indians protested that if they acted as intermediaries for the American government, they might well be killed, but they agreed to remain neutral. War continued on the frontier. The Americans won the Battle of Fallen Timbers against the Ohio Indians, at least partially due to the neutrality of the Six Nations.

In 1794 Knox resigned as secretary of war, and Washington appointed Pickering to the post, since it mostly involved dealing with Indians. He accepted the position because he had no other income. He had become one of the first professional politicians. But never satisfied and always thinking he knew better than others, he became a troublemaker.

In 1795 John Jay negotiated a treaty with the British that included their evacuating the forts on the frontier, a move Pickering wanted. It would remove British agitation of the Indians. Washington and most of his Cabinet were in favor of ratification, despite the protests of Thomas Jefferson and his followers, who wanted a closer relationship with France.

Secretary of State Edmund Randolph opposed ratification of the treaty, and Pickering set out to undermine him. He had some letters from the French minister to Randolph, which had come into possession of the British and been passed to Pickering. The letters suggested that Randolph had asked for a bribe from the French to stir up civil war in America. This would help France, which was at war with England.

When the Cabinet ended its debate on the Jay Treaty, Washington decided to ratify, against Randolph's advice. Pickering then accused Randolph of treason. Randolph briefly defended himself but then resigned.

Pickering was made acting secretary of state while Washington offered the post to six others, who rejected it. Alexander Hamilton lamented that there was "no first-rate man" available, which he thought was "a sad omen for the government." Washington's first administration had included the best minds in America, but now the candidates for Cabinet posts had deteriorated to such people as Pickering, Hamilton thought.

Pickering was furious and humiliated that the position had been offered to six others first, but he accepted anyway.

He was a poor choice for a diplomat. He was unable to compromise or to shrug off criticism, and he turned small disagreements into huge moral issues. His actions almost led to war with France in 1796 and to a Jeffersonian victory in that year. The French foreign minister, Pierre Adet, published a letter he had sent to Pickering criticizing the Federalist government for failing to protect its neutrality and allowing Britain to seize its ships and impress its sailors. Since he had twice written Pickering about the matter and been ignored, Adet wrote, France would now allow privateers to seize American ships.

President Washington was astounded, and demanded to know if the charges were true. Pickering admitted that he had not responded to Adet's letters since the charges were offensive. Worse, he had withheld the letters from the president. The election for president was days away, and there must be some response, or the Federalists would lose. Unfortunately, Washington allowed Pickering to write and publish a letter without taking the time to read it himself. It only made matters worse. Pickering wrote that there was no such law as freedom of the seas, that Britain was justified in seizing American ships carrying French goods, and that it was none of France's business what America did.

Hamilton advised Washington to "avoid a rupture" with France by writing a conciliatory but not humbling letter to the American minister in France. When the letter was composed, after many drafts that mentioned the long history of good relations between France and America, Washington sent it to Hamilton, not Pickering, for approval.

The breach with France was healed, but the Republicans pilloried Pickering, as well they should. But Pickering didn't learn from this misstep. Moreover, he never assumed the blame for what he had done but laid it on others. Washington, he wrote, was "a much overrated, semi-literate mediocrity, whose aides had saved him during the Revolution and whose brilliant Cabinet ministers had made his first administration a triumph." He said nothing about the second administration, of which he was a part.

When John Adams narrowly won election to be president in 1796, several Federalists advised him to remove Pickering as secretary of state to improve relations with France. It was good advice, but Adams did not follow it. First, he was not sure he had the power to fire a Cabinet officer whom he had not appointed. The tradition of completely changing officials with each new administration had not developed. Second, he thought that getting rid of Pickering—which the French wanted—would indicate weakness. Moreover, he saw that the country was divided in its foreign loyalties, so he needed to keep good relations with both Britain and France.

Pickering thought he could manage Adams better than he had Washington, and he pushed for war with France.

America's representatives in London and in Berlin were aghast. Napoleon was at the peak of his conquests in Europe, and the coalition against him was crumbling. The French would be masters of Europe and of the seas, so it was not a good time to take them on as enemies.

Adams decided to send a peace commission to Paris and chose John Marshall, Charles Cotesworth Pinckney, and Eldridge Gerry as its members. Although Gerry had been a friend and colleague for years, Pickering objected to him as "not Federalist enough," which was precisely why Adams had chosen him; he wanted someone neutral. When word came that the commissioners had been refused permission to speak to the French minister, in what was called the XYZ Affair, Pickering wrote the details to Hamilton before he released the information to President Adams, a clear case of disloyalty. Pickering wanted war with France and an alliance with Britain.

Marshall and Pinckney returned, but Gerry remained in Paris. He sent a letter saying that Talleyrand, the French prime minister warned that if he left, France would declare war.

Pickering thought the French might attack our western region through Louisiana or stir up a slave revolt in the Southern states. He saw conspiracies everywhere and pushed Adams to raise an army with the aging and ill Washington in charge and Hamilton second in command.

Then Gerry came home with a letter from Talleyrand saying that the French wanted peace. Gerry published it, along with his comment that he thought Talleyrand was sincere. Pickering published a rebuke of Gerry, first claiming that the French had duped Gerry and then that Gerry had collaborated with Talleyrand.

Adams knew the American people didn't want war or the high taxes that went along with it, and he decided to send Williams Van Murray to negotiate with the French. Pickering wrote letters to Federalist leaders criticizing Adams and organized a protest of the mission to France. Adams agreed not to send Van Murray unless he had assurances from the French that the envoy would be well received.

When assurances came, Adams asked Pickering to write out the envoy's instructions promptly. Pickering wrote out terms for the mission so demanding they would not be accepted, and Secretary of War James McHenry tried to convince Van Murray not to send his dispatches to President Adams but to Pickering. Pickering also pushed Adams to delay the mission, but finally the president went ahead with his plans.

Pickering, seeing that he could not control Adams, wrote letters to Federalists urging them to drop Adams as a candidate for president in 1800 "to save the country from ruin." He charged that Adams was conspiring to become a Republican and be Jefferson's vice president.

Finally, Adams had had enough of Pickering's double dealing. When Pickering refused the president's request to resign, Adams fired him.

Pickering went to his Pennsylvania land and cleared a few acres but found "pioneering" was not easy. His friends raised funds to purchase some of his worthless land and buy him a small farm near Salem, Massachusetts, so he could support his family, but they would not give him money.

Pickering ran for the House of Representatives from Essex County in 1800, but lost, as most Federalists did. Then in 1802 the legislature appointed John Quincy Adams to a six-year term as U.S. senator and Pickering to serve the remaining two years of the term of a senator who resigned. Pickering was back in government, but still haughty and harsh. He didn't cooperate with other Federalists in the Senate and especially hated young Adams.

Pickering was not appointed to any important committees and in return he made bitter, critical speeches. He accused Jefferson of planning to become "president for life," thought the Louisiana Purchase was made to give power to slave states, and wanted the New England states to secede and form a separate nation. He wanted Aaron Burr to be governor of New York in the new nation he was planning, which he would probably have insisted on naming "Pickering." He asked Hamilton to head up his new nation's army, but Hamilton refused.

Despite his behavior, Pickering was reelected in 1804.

Britain was still seizing American ships and impressing our sailors, but Pickering insisted that France was doing worse and we should accept the situation with Britain. He submitted a letter to the Massachusetts legislature saying that Jefferson was under the control of the French and that the embargo, which kept Americans from trading with Britain and France, was really meant to punish New England, which needed British trade. Pickering also published the letter in a newspaper, and it was spread throughout America. He was widely criticized for trying to "disunite, divide, and dissolve the nation." This coincided with discussion on repealing the embargo. The British minister announced that discussions between the two nations had broken down.

Jefferson turned over documents to be read in the Senate indicating that there was no evidence of French control of him or the American government and that America, not Britain, had broken off negotiations. Pickering was dismayed. He had been wrong, though he would not admit it.

Republicans loved to antagonize Pickering. He was so extreme in his views that he made the perfect opponent. Oddly enough, his colleagues censured him not for an absurd remark, but for reading aloud in the Senate from a document that was supposed to have been kept secret.

He was defeated for reelection to the Senate in 1810 but elected to the House of Representatives in 1812, when America was at war—with Britain, not France, as he had hoped. When a rumor spread that Russia had offered to negotiate peace, Pickering claimed it was a hoax of the Madison administration. President James Madison produced documents to prove that the rumor was true. Madison said he and the British were in talks in 1814 to end the war, but Pickering thought it was just a screen to continue the war, which New England opposed. When Vice President Eldridge Gerry died, Pickering refused to join in a resolution honoring him, because Gerry had become a Republican! Yet Pickering himself had repeatedly changed loyalties throughout his life, and would again.

In 1824, because Pickering hated John Quincy Adams, the Federalist candidate for president, he switched sides and supported Adams's opponent, Democrat Andrew Jackson. When people complained that Jackson was not "learned," Pickering said learning was not essential to being president. "George Washington and James Monroe proved that," he declared.

Pickering began writing a history of the United States, in which he spoke of "Washington's mediocrity, Adams's vanity, and Jefferson's hypocrisy." Bitter to the last, he never finished the history. He died in 1829, aged eighty-three.

SOURCES

I had never heard of Timothy Pickering until I began researching this book. Then once I encountered his name, it showed up often in biographies of the other famous men of early America. He had a grudge against most of them and deliberately tried to undermine the foreign policy of both Washington and Adams.

Gerard H. Clarfield is the recognized scholar on Timothy Pickering. I read both of his books on Pickering: *Timothy Pickering and American Diplomacy 1795–1800* (Columbia: The University of Missouri Press, 1969) and *Timothy Pickering and the American Republic* (Pittsburgh, Pa.: University of Pittsburgh Press, 1980). Pickering is also prominently mentioned in Leonard D. White's *The Federalists* (New York: Macmillan Company, 1956); Gore Vidal's *Inventing a Nation* (New Haven, Conn.: Yale University Press, 2003); Edward J. Larson's *A Magnificent Catastrophe: The Tumultuous Election of 1800* (New York: Simon & Schuster, 2007); and *Crisis in Freedom—The Alien and Sedition Acts* by John C. Miller (Boston: Little, Brown and Company, 1951).

CHAPTER THREE

The Cases against Aaron Burr: *Murder, Treason, or Just Bad Judgment?*

Aaron Burr's name is one of the most recognized in American history, not for his accomplishments, which were many, but for the bad things he did. At least three times in his political life, when he faced a crucial decision, he behaved as a jerk.

Burr is remembered most for having shot and killed Alexander Hamilton in a famous duel. Yet other men who killed during a duel were not scorned as Burr was. Later, he stood in the dock in federal court in Richmond, Virginia, accused of treason for trying to seize the newly purchased Louisiana Territory, Florida and Mexico, and set up a kingdom with himself as ruler. He was acquitted, but the shadow of the charge never left him. He had earlier come close to being elected president of the United States, in 1800, tied with Thomas Jefferson. His election could have changed the history of America, keeping Federalists in control for another decade. The poor choices he made prevented him from ever having another opportunity to run for the presidency.

Aaron Burr was born in 1756 with what we would now call "a silver spoon in his mouth." He was the second child and first son of the president of the College of New Jersey (later Princeton). Aaron's grandfather was the famous theologian Jonathan Edwards. It seemed that life would go smoothly for young Aaron. Then, when he was only two, his father died. His grandfather Edwards took over as college president, only to die soon afterward following an inoculation for smallpox. Aaron's mother and grandmother also died within a few months. The orphaned Aaron and his sister, Sally, were declared the wards of their twenty-one-year-old uncle,

Aaron Burr was the only vice president ever accused of either murder or treason—
and he was sought for both.

Timothy Edwards. Aaron became a troublemaker, running away, destroying property, and acting out his grief and confusion. His youthful guardian laughed off Aaron's escapades and made little effort to discipline him.

When Aaron was eleven, he asked to be admitted to the College of New Jersey but was refused. The brilliant, precocious youth set about educating himself and two years later was admitted to the college as a sophomore. He achieved high grades and graduated at sixteen, but while he was vaguely ambitious, he had no real career interest. He hung around college for a year following his graduation, supported by his uncle, then spent a year studying for the ministry, before finally deciding to become a lawyer.

The coming of the Revolutionary War changed the course of his life. He left the study of law, joined the Continental Army, and was made a captain at nineteen. He went along with General Benedict Arnold on the grueling but successful attack on Quebec, and when one of his commanding officers, General Richard Montgomery, fell in battle, Burr carried his body off the battlefield and rallied the disorganized troops. Returning from Canada in triumph, he was posted to General George Washington's army and was with Washington at Germantown. He became a lieutenant colonel, a title he retained the rest of his life.

Despite his rapid rise, the military life was not to his liking, and his attitude was not to Washington's liking. When Burr was promoted, he wrote to Washington, not thanking him but protesting the tardiness of the promotion. He claimed that he had better plans for carrying on the war than Washington, whom he considered just a plain country farmer, uneducated and unsuited for high office. Burr was already showing the arrogance and the sense of entitlement that would lead him to make erroneous decisions. Offending Washington was definitely a poor decision. In 1779, he claimed that ill health due to headaches required him to take a leave of absence from military service. This was heresy to Washington, who had endured dreadful conditions as leader of the army and would go on doing so. He gave curt permission for Burr to resign.

Burr's jealousy of Alexander Hamilton, which was to bedevil him the remainder of his life, may have begun at this time. Hamilton, also young and brilliant, had caught the attention of General Washington, who would be elected president, while Burr's commander, Benedict Arnold, had gone down in disgrace. Washington made Hamilton his aide and treated him like a son. (In some rumors, Hamilton was Washington's son, conceived when the general had visited his brother in the West Indies, but this is extremely unlikely, since Washington never fathered any children by his fertile wife, Martha, who had four children in her first marriage.) Hamilton handled the financial matters of the army, becoming a general, and later as the first secretary of the treasury, was the financial genius of the American government. In the Washington administration, there was no position for Burr.

Neither military service nor frequent headaches kept Burr from leading an active social life, including his courtship of Theodosia Prevost. She was a decade older than Burr, the mother of four children and married to a military officer serving in Jamaica. Soon after word came of her husband's death, the widow married Burr.

The couple had four children, but only one survived infancy, a daughter also named Theodosia.

Burr became partner in a New York law firm and attracted the attention of powerful people in the state. He considered himself a Federalist and worked with Hamilton to unseat George Clinton, the longtime governor of New York. New York City politics were split into factions, the Clintons, the Livingstons, and the Dutch patroons led by Alexander Hamilton's father-in-law, Philip Schuyler. Clinton won reelection by a narrow margin, and when the post of attorney general became vacant, he appointed Aaron Burr— partly as revenge against Hamilton, partly to keep Burr too occupied to seek the office of governor himself. Burr managed at this point to remain independent, with supporters among both the Federalists and the up-and-coming Republicans, led by Thomas Jefferson.

As attorney general of New York, Burr was also land agent for the state. In that position he sold over three million acres of western land to Alexander Macomb, a New York merchant, for eight cents an acre. Burr himself, though always broke, managed to buy one hundred thousand acres of land. Where did he get the money? The Burrs lived lavishly, and he often gave money to friends when he was himself in debt. This somewhat suspicious land deal was the first of many troublesome acts that would eventually destroy his reputation.

Burr disagreed with Hamilton on political issues, and a certain amount of jealousy persisted between the two men. They were close in age, both orphaned as children, and both determined to achieve prominence on the national stage. Eager to ingratiate himself with Jefferson, Burr is believed to have joined Jefferson in "setting up" Hamilton with Maria Reynolds, wife of a currency speculator. Hamilton might have resisted her charming pleas for help, but the conspirators knew their man. He had an affair with Maria that tarnished his reputation, not because of the woman herself, but because of her husband. When James Reynolds was found guilty of speculating in government bonds and cheating the original buyers, suspicion fell on Hamilton for having provided Reynolds with inside information. Soon Burr acted as Maria's lawyer in divorcing her husband.

Having an affair at that time was not cause for much criticism. After Burr's wife, Theodosia, died of cancer in 1794, he had a series of affairs, and in his correspondence are notes from women asking for money and mentioning pregnancies. Burr may or may not have been the father, but he soon had the reputation as a womanizer.

Burr's eleven-year-old daughter Theodosia acted as her father's hostess during the frequent entertaining at the Burr mansion, Richmond Hill. For the rest of her life, he treated her as an equal, writing her letters about his affairs with various women and reporting intimate details of his life. For example, he reported on his progress in his ultimately unsuccessful attempt to marry a wealthy woman, referred to as "Madame D."

Burr was as ambitious as he was charming. He wanted a higher office than attorney general—perhaps U.S. senator. Governor Clinton appointed Burr to be a U.S. senator, and Clinton continued as governor, serving seven three-year terms. By this time, George Washington had retired to Mount Vernon, and John Adams, a Federalist, was president. Hamilton had resigned and returned to practice law in New York. Burr thus was freed from both his rival and the leader he felt contempt for. He managed to be popular in the Senate with both Federalists and Republicans. At the same time, he was a secret agent for the French government, cooperating with the Directory, a group that ran the government before Napoleon assumed control.

The election of 1800 was the high point of Burr's political career. In four years it would crash. Thomas Jefferson, a Republican, had every intention of becoming president in 1800. So did Burr and several others. Even Adams thought he might serve a second term.

When the electoral votes were counted, Adams was odd man out, and Jefferson and Burr were tied. According to the Constitution, a tied election was to be decided by the House of Representatives, with each state having one vote. When the House convened in January 1801 to break the tie, it took over thirty ballots before one of the New York representatives who had supported Burr decided that Jefferson was more trustworthy. Burr was left with the vice presidency.

If Burr had asked his supporters early in the balloting to cast their votes for Jefferson, he might have earned Jefferson's gratitude and become the heir apparent. But he didn't, confident he could win the presidency on his own. A vindictive Jefferson relegated Burr to an inactive position, turned down his requests for political appointments for some of his supporters, and instead pushed the political futures of his Virginia followers, Madison and Monroe. By trying to stay independent of both the Republicans and the Federalists, Burr had achieved nothing.

As president of the Senate, he was called upon to cast a tie-breaking vote when the Jeffersonians wanted to repeal the

Judiciary Act of 1801. This act had created additional judgeships, filled by Federalists appointed by Adams, and the Republicans wanted the judges removed. Federalists and Republicans were evenly divided in the Senate. Burr hesitated. If he had voted no, the Federalists might have supported him for the presidency in 1804, but he voted yes and earned their ire. In a later proposed revision of the act, he voted with the Federalists, and thus angered the Republicans. Again, by trying to appease both parties, he had alienated both.

Seeing few political opportunities for himself in Washington, Burr visited his daughter, Theodosia, now married to a South Carolinian, and was there when his beloved grandson and namesake, Aaron Burr Alston, was born. On his return he detoured through "the Floridas," an area that included present-day Florida and territory as far west as New Orleans. Florida was controlled by Spain, and France had just sold Louisiana to the United States.

Burr began to consider a deal with Spain, or with Britain, to separate part of the southern territory and set up a new nation. The New England states, chafing under the domination of Jefferson and the Virginians, were calling for the secession of New England and New York. If they could do so, why not an additional nation on the southern border? This nation could even challenge Spanish control of Mexico and expand southward.

Back in Washington, Burr faced a challenge to his reputation. He had been accused of fraud and treason by James Cheetham, a "yellow journalist," in what was called the Pamphlet War. Burr was slow to respond, so the stories about him took on a life of their own, spreading throughout the nation.

Burr was primed for a fight. All he lacked was a target, and Alexander Hamilton inadvertently provided that. Hamilton had long criticized Burr, and been ignored, but this time he went too far. A guest at a party wrote a letter to a newspaper editor claiming that Hamilton had said Burr was guilty of "a despicable act." Several sources concluded that the charge was incest, beginning when Burr's daughter was only nine. This charge was too damning to be ignored. Burr demanded an apology.

Instead, Hamilton replied that he couldn't remember exactly what he had said when. It was a lawyer's defense, but not one that would satisfy Burr. Burr demanded that Hamilton deny all the accusations he had ever made against Burr. When the denial was not forthcoming, Burr challenged Hamilton to a duel.

Early on the morning of July 11, 1804, the two men and their seconds met at Weehawken, New Jersey, as dueling was illegal in New York. Hamilton had planned to fire wide of the mark and probably did, but Burr shot with deadly accuracy. Shots rang out, and Hamilton fell. He was taken home and died soon after.

Burr had badly erred in killing Hamilton. He had let his anger and jealousy overcome his sense. Masses turned out for Hamilton's funeral, and Burr found himself charged with murder in New Jersey and New York. He was a fugitive on the run. No vice president before or since has been so charged. Strangely, he was never tried for Hamilton's killing.

Burr had given Jefferson a perfect reason to drop him from the presidential ticket in the election of 1804. The method of choosing the top officeholders had changed, so that two of the same party ran together, opposing two of another party. Burr appealed to Jefferson to choose him, but Jefferson was noncommittal. He suddenly showered appointments on Burr's followers but chose as his running mate George Clinton, still governor of New York and known as the "Old Incumbent." The Old Incumbent would be a placeholder, never a challenge to Jefferson, while Burr might have been.

Aaron Burr's political life was over. He returned to preside over the Senate one last time in the impeachment trial of Supreme Court Justice Samuel Chase. Burr handled the trial with such dignity that his departure from the Senate chamber afterward was a somber, moving moment.

But Burr was not walking off the national stage. He headed west, to the recently purchased Louisiana Territory. Here he could make a new start. He conferred with the British minister, Anthony Merry, promising to help Britain in its war with France, in return for 110,000 pounds sterling and the support of the British fleet off New Orleans. Merry agreed to contact the British government. Nothing came of this, but Burr did have the financial support of his son-in-law, Joseph Alston, who contributed $50,000 to the enterprise.

Burr visited Andrew Jackson in Tennessee and was feted at a ball, as the most famous American to visit the west. He met with Harman Blennerhassett, who owned an island at a strategic point on the Mississippi River, and with James Wilkinson, the highest-ranking general in the American army and a former comrade of Burr's. Unknown to Burr, Wilkinson was also a paid spy for Spain.

President Jefferson was warned of the plot but took no action until Wilkinson himself turned in Burr. Jefferson had Burr arrested and brought to Richmond to be tried for treason. Here as in Tennessee, Burr was popular, even having dinner with Chief Justice John Marshall, who was to preside at his trial. Burr was defended by some of the most prominent lawyers of the time, including Edmund Randolph, a former attorney general, and Luther Martin, a signer of the Declaration of Independence and a longtime friend. Andrew Jackson was among the crowd attending the trial.

Jefferson, claiming executive privilege, refused to turn over the letters Wilkinson had written to him, and Wilkinson's testimony was suspect. Jefferson had appointed Wilkinson governor of northern Louisiana, a position Wilkinson exploited. He was reprimanded for his harsh treatment of the inhabitants and was later court-martialed for his actions.

In his instructions to the jurors, Chief Justice Marshall reminded them that treason required an overt act and two witnesses to the act, not merely a plan or intention. There were no overt acts and no uninvolved witnesses. The jury had no choice but to find Burr not guilty.

Whether guilty or not, Burr had again acted as a jerk. Had he acted in the same manner a generation later, he would have been considered a patriot like Sam Houston, who took Mexican territory and set up a separate republic.

After the trial, Burr traveled to England, where he was considered *persona non grata* and ordered to leave. He went to Sweden and then to France, hoping to cooperate with Napoleon in seizing not only Mexico from Spain, but also Jamaica and Canada from the British. The French distrusted him and put him under house arrest. He escaped and arrived back in America in 1811, when war with the British was imminent.

A capable lawyer, Burr soon had a group of well-paying clients, but his troubles were not over.

His grandson, Aaron Burr Alston, died suddenly. Then his daughter, Theodosia, on her way from South Carolina to visit her father, was lost when the vessel she was sailing on was shipwrecked.

In gratitude for Luther Martin's loyalty and strong defense of him in his treason trial, Burr took in the feeble old man and supported him until his death in 1826.

In 1833, the seventy-seven-year-old Burr married Eliza Bowen Jumel, one of the wealthiest women in America. It was an unhappy marriage. Mrs. Burr sued him for divorce a year later, on the grounds that he was an adulterer! He died on the day the divorce decree was to be granted.

Sources

Much has been written about Aaron Burr, most of it defamatory. Burr was involved with the major political figures of his time, especially Thomas Jefferson and Alexander Hamilton, and I relied on biographies of these two men as well as of Burr himself.

Sources consulted include the following: *Colonel Aaron Burr, the American Phoenix*, by Samuel Engle Burr Jr. (New York: Exposition Press, 1961); *Thomas Jefferson* by Thomas J. Fleming (New York: Grosset & Dunlap, 1969); *Hamilton II 1789–1804* by Robert A. Hendrickson (New York: Mason/Charter Books, 1976). Also by Hendrickson, *The Rise and Fall of Alexander Hamilton* (New

York: Van Nostrand Reinhold Company, 1981); *Forgotten Founder, Drunken Prophet: The Life of Luther Martin*, by Bill Kaufman (Wilmington, Del.: ISI Books, 2008); *Burr, Hamilton and Jefferson*, by Roger G. Kennedy (New York: Oxford University Press, 2000); *Aaron Burr—The Years from Princeton to Vice President 1756–1805*, by Milton Lomask (New York: Farrar, Strauss & Giroux, 1979); *Aaron Burr, Conspiracy to Treason* by Buckner F. Melton (New York: John Wiley & Sons, 2001); *The Democratic Republic 1801–1815* by Marshall Smelser (New York: Harper & Row Publishers, 1968); and *Jefferson's Vendetta* by Joseph Wheelan (New York: Carroll & Graf Publishers, 2005).

Samuel Chase was not an impartial justice—he was a Federalist.

CHAPTER FOUR

The Impeachment
of Samuel Chase

Justice Samuel Chase behaved badly in court, speculated in land deals, and was undoubtedly a jerk in a number of ways. He was impeached, however, not for his outbursts and improper instructions to juries, but because he was a Federalist, and Thomas Jefferson hated Federalists, especially Federalists in the judiciary.

Chase, the son of an Episcopal minister, was born in Somerset County, Maryland, in 1741. He was educated at home by his father, and at age eighteen, he went to Annapolis to study law. Two years later he was admitted to the bar and set up a law practice. In 1762, only twenty-one years old, he married Ann Baldwin. Marriage, however, did not settle him down. That year he was expelled from the Forensics Club, a debating society in Annapolis, for "extremely irregular and indecent behavior." This was the first of many public criticisms of his opinions and behavior.

For a few years, Chase led an uneventful life as far as politics were concerned. He and Ann had seven children, only four of whom survived to adulthood. In 1764 he was elected to the Maryland House of Delegates.

Trouble was brewing between England and her American colonies, and when Parliament passed the Stamp Act in 1765, Chase and his friend William Paca cofounded the Anne Arundel County chapter of the Sons of Liberty. The Sons of Liberty kept the colonists aware of events happening in the other colonies, but the group also broke into stamp sellers' offices and destroyed the stamps.

Chase was one of four Maryland delegates to the Continental Congress, meeting in Philadelphia, and after the Revolutionary War began, he was sent to Canada along with Benjamin Franklin and several others, in an attempt to persuade the Canadians to join the rebellion against Britain. They misjudged the Canadians, who declined to join, and who demanded payment in gold, not American paper money, for any services furnished to the delegation.

Chase was a signer of the Declaration of Independence and was a widely respected man with a bright future. However, like many of the Founding Fathers, he had financial problems. His wife, Ann, died about 1776, leaving him with four young children. When his father died, Samuel Chase also took over the responsibility of four children from his father's second marriage. He had regularly speculated in land and bought confiscated British property. He borrowed to purchase and then had to sell to repay the loan. He needed money.

Chase was accused of taking advantage of his position in the Continental Congress to corner the market in wheat flour furnished to the Continental Army. The charges were not proved, but he was not reelected to the Continental Congress in 1778 because of lingering suspicion of war profiteering.

In 1784 Chase was sent to England as attorney for the state of Maryland, to get the money Maryland had invested in the Bank of England before the Revolutionary War. If the money was not reclaimed, it would become crown property. The bank trustees held the deposit subject to payment for British property seized in Maryland, so he was not successful in getting the money. It was two decades before the matter was finally settled and Chase was paid his fee and reimbursed for his expenses. A more immediate benefit to Chase, however, was meeting and marrying his second wife, Hannah Kitty.

In 1786 the Chase family moved to Baltimore. In 1788 he was appointed chief justice of the District Criminal Court in Baltimore and three years later, he was named chief justice of the Maryland General Court as well. He thus held two appointed jobs at once, in another attempt to increase his income, but it was a conflict of interest. Instead of removing Chase as his enemies requested, the Maryland legislature eventually abolished the lower court position.

Chase's political opinions changed gradually from the "firebrand of the Revolution," as he was called earlier, to a more conservative stance. Although he at first opposed ratification of the Constitution, he later became one of its staunchest supporters. He thought that the national government needed stabilizing and strengthening. Jefferson's followers believed that President Washington's government was too much like the British system and was representative of the propertied class—though most Jeffersonians were themselves owners of large property.

In 1796, Washington nominated Chase to be an associate justice of the Supreme Court, a position that then had little prestige and was indeed a grueling job. Few cases required the attention of the justices in the national capital, but each justice was assigned a circuit and was expected to "ride the circuit." This meant that for much of the year, the justice would be going from county to county within his district, hearing cases alongside a local judge.

Chase was a justice when Congress passed the Alien and Sedition Acts. Britain and France were at war in Europe, and both nations were attacking American ships. French immigrants urged a strong alliance between the United States and France as payment for France's help in winning American independence. Britain, despite conceding American independence, still kept troops in forts in the Northwest Territory and seized American sailors to serve in the British navy.

When John Jay returned from a mission to Britain with a treaty that granted few of America's demands and sent most "to arbitration," leading Federalists were criticized and President John Adams was burned in effigy.

Sentiment turned against the French when American diplomats returned from Paris to report that three members of the French Directory had demanded a huge bribe for dealing with our representatives.

Recent immigrants and citizens took sides. No matter whether the government was pro-French or pro-British, complaints made headlines in all the newspapers, and President Adams said that he could have traveled from Philadelphia to Boston at night, his way lighted by bonfires where he was burned in effigy.

To stop criticism, Congress passed the Alien and Sedition Acts, a series of measures that raised the residency requirement for immigrants to become American citizens and allowed the president to deport any aliens who were suspected of working against the government. In the sections that caused the most protest, however, it became a crime to criticize the president, and treason now included not just aiding the enemy, but interfering with the enforcement of federal laws. In addition, to build up our navy in preparation for possible war, a House Tax was passed to raise the necessary funds. It was levied against all households, the amount to be determined by assessors.

The first case under the Alien and Sedition Acts was brought against a Pennsylvania resident, John Fries. There was widespread anger at the House Tax, and a group of protesters had kidnapped a tax assessor and physically abused him, thus resisting a law of the United States. This constituted treason. Troops were called, and a number of rebels were arrested. Fries and several hundred "insurrectionists" marched to the prison at Bethlehem, Pennsylvania, and forced the marshals to release the prisoners.

At the first trial of Fries, Supreme Court Justice James Iredell presided. He read out the terms of the Sedition Act, and the jury concluded that Fries and his two fellow defendants were guilty of treason. On the day of sentencing, the defense attorney moved for a new trial on the grounds that one of the jurors was prejudiced against Fries. Since the penalty for treason was death, it was important that he have a fair trial.

At the second trial, Justice Chase presided along with Judge Richard Peters. Again Fries was found guilty, together with his two coconspirators. In sentencing Fries, Chase delivered a stinging indictment of the defendant's actions: Living in the freest country in the world, Fries had been discontented to the point of wickedness and folly in rebelling against the government. His punishment would be an example to others who opposed the lawful government of the United States. Fries should repent and in his remaining few days of life might see a minister of the Gospel if he liked.

As it turned out, Fries had not a few days of life left, but eighteen more years. He and his fellow conspirators were pardoned by President Adams.

Soon Chase was sent to preside in the libel trial of James Callender in Richmond, Virginia. Callender was accused of libeling President John Adams by publishing the book, *The Prospect Before Us*, with financial support from Thomas Jefferson. Chase's longtime friend, attorney Luther Martin, had given Chase a copy of the booklet, with what Martin considered the libelous passages underlined. Chase had it with him on the stagecoach trip to Richmond and commented to a fellow passenger that it was a pity Virginia had not already disposed of the scoundrel who wrote it. This later came up in court as indicating that Chase had prejudged the defendant, who was found guilty of defaming President Adams and was sentenced to nine months in jail and assessed a $200 fine. Adams did not pardon him.

Before the election of 1800, Chase campaigned throughout Maryland for the reelection of Adams, and his absence from the Supreme Court meant the justices did not have a quorum. Thus no cases could be heard.

His campaigning was in vain. Republicans won the presidency and control of the House of Representatives, swept to victory by public anger against the Sedition Act. The Senate was divided, 15-15.

Before Jefferson, the new president, and Congress took office, President Adams and the Federalist-controlled Congress passed the Judiciary Act of 1801, creating many new federal judgeships and filling them all with Federalists appointed by Adams in the last hours of his administration. With the new judges in place, the justices would no longer have to ride the circuit.

Jefferson was furious. He set out to end Federalist control of the judiciary. His first step was to repeal the Judiciary Act of 1801. There were no judgeships for Jefferson to fill with loyal

Republicans, as those positions no longer existed, but neither were there numerous Federalist judges installed for life.

Jefferson pardoned all who had been convicted under the Sedition Act. The Sedition Act itself had expired at the end of Adams's term.

Jefferson next turned to removing sitting judges and justices. His ultimate target was probably his cousin John Marshall, chief justice of the Supreme Court, the most Federalist of all the Federalists. In the meantime, there were others for whom Jefferson could find more obvious reasons for removal. District Judge John Pickering of New Hampshire was an alcoholic and insane as well. During the time that the Judiciary Act of 1801 was in effect, a provision in the act made it possible for a substitute judge to serve in his place, but that no longer applied. The judge would not resign. The impeachment process, Jefferson told U.S. Senator William Plumer of New Hampshire, was a "bungling method," but it would have to do. The Constitution provided that officials might be impeached and removed for "high crimes and misdemeanors," not drunkenness and insanity. Jefferson thought that the president, with the consent of Congress, should be able to remove a member of the judiciary for any reason—or no reason.

The impeachment went forward, and the Senate found Judge Pickering guilty. He was removed from office, and his successor was a Republican who had led the effort to get rid of the judge.

If impeachment had worked to remove a helpless judge, might it be the way to get rid of Justice Samuel Chase? He was neither insane nor an alcoholic, but he had made enemies because of his courtroom manner. He felt free to express his opinion, and when presiding in Baltimore, he claimed that repeal of the Judiciary Act of 1801 had altered the nature of justice. In addition, he criticized his state, Maryland, for having declared universal suffrage without regard to property. This, he said, would destroy the legal protection of property and lead to "mobocracy" as the government of the United States.

Chase thus became a target for Jefferson.

Jefferson wrote Joseph Nicholson, a congressman from Maryland, suggesting impeachment for Chase for his "seditious . . . attack on the principles of the Constitution." He indicated that "the public will look" to Congress for punishment of Chase. As usual, Jefferson covered his actions by concluding, "For myself, it is better that I not interfere," though he had done just that.

In 1792, Jefferson, acting through his friend, Congressman William Branch Giles, had brought impeachment charges against Secretary of the Treasury Alexander Hamilton, accusing him of failing to account for federal funds. Giles tried to trap Hamilton by demanding a huge number of official papers in a short time. Hamilton managed to produce them. Jefferson then charged Hamilton in the Senate, but Hamilton was vindicated. Jefferson later wrote that he "did not recollect" anything of the matter.

He had lost the battle with Hamilton, but this time he was sure he could win.

Chase's trial began on February 4, 1805, shortly before Jefferson began his second term as president. Congressman John Randolph, usually referred to as John Randolph of Roanoke, the name of his plantation in Virginia, brought charges as majority leader in the House of Representatives. The Senate would be the jury. Presiding was Vice President Aaron Burr, shortly to be out of office, and under a charge of murder by New Jersey and New York for killing Hamilton. A contemporary said of the proceedings that usually a murderer is brought before a judge for trial. In this case, the judge was brought before the murderer.

The Senate chamber was decorated with colorful bunting: A section was marked off in red for the senators who would judge, in much the manner of British courts. Three rows of seats covered in green were for the members of the House of Representatives, and a special section with chairs and desks covered in blue were for the managers of the prosecution and the lawyers for Chase's defense. The spectators' gallery was crowded.

The defendant was a massive man, tall and imposing, with a mane of white hair and a ruddy face that earned him the nickname,

"Old Bacon Face." His lead attorney, Luther Martin of Maryland, had also been a signer of the Declaration of Independence and was a lifelong friend of Chase's. Martin, despite his slovenly appearance, poor speaking voice, and occasional inebriation before the court, was recognized as a brilliant lawyer.

Opposing them, John Randolph was tall and emaciated, with the pale beardless face of a youth, due to a condition that also rendered him impotent. He strode the Senate chamber as he talked, wearing boots and cracking a whip. Despite his appearance and his reedy voice, he was a commanding figure in the House. He had a brilliant mind but was disliked by some of his Republican colleagues because of his bullying ways. He was a cousin of President Jefferson and Chief Justice John Marshall.

Randolph began his presentation by comparing the courtroom behavior of Chase with that of Marshall, whom he described as quiet and well-mannered. However, Chase was not being charged with poor manners but with statements and rulings that made it difficult for those who appeared before his court to get a fair trial.

The first charge related to the Fries case. Fries's lawyers claimed that at the beginning of the trial Chase had presented them with a written statement of what the law was: Since the United States was not at war, Fries could not be charged with aiding and abetting the enemy. But refusing to obey a federal law and interfering with federal officers could be construed as treason. (Today, Fries would probably be charged with "obstruction of justice," not treason.) The court therefore needed only to be presented with the facts of the case. Judges often summarize the applicable law when they instruct the jury at the end of a trial, but not before any testimony is given. The defense lawyers protested that they should have the right to argue the constitutionality of the law as well as the facts and refused to further represent Fries.

The following day Chase relented and said that they could argue the law as well as the facts, but the defense lawyers objected that while Chase might dispense with the paper he'd written his opinion on, he "could not erase from his mind" his interpretation of the law. Privately, they thought their client would do better to throw himself on the mercy of the court, without legal representation. Members of the Pennsylvania bar agreed that Chase's interpretation of the law was accurate, and it coincided with what had been put forward in Fries's earlier trial. To most legal scholars, Chase had not erred, but Randolph and the Republicans were out for Chase's blood.

In the Callender libel case, Chase was charged with the following offenses: First, he refused to allow Callender a continuance—or postponement—until the next term of court, only a delay of several weeks to allow him time to summon witnesses. Second, Chase allowed a juror to be seated who stated that he believed *Prospect* was inflammatory and libelous, having seen abstracts of it in a Richmond newspaper. Third, Chase had refused to allow Colonel John Taylor to be called as a witness and questioned, but rather required that questions for Taylor be put in writing. Fourth, Chase harangued the defense counsel.

Chase's defense argued that since Chase was presiding alongside another judge in all cases, if Chase were guilty, then so should the other judges be.

Chase's failure to grant a continuance was dismissed as a charge. Judges were within their rights to grant them or not. The defense argued that Chase had ruled in the case of the juror that it was the book as a whole and not an excerpt that was the basis for the case. As to Taylor's testimony, Chase demanded what the defense intended to prove, a question judges often ask. Taylor could prove the truth of one of the charges made in the book, defense counsel answered. Again Chase ruled that it was the entire book that was considered libelous, and disproving a small portion did not change the tenor of the case.

As in the Fries case, Chase was charged with not allowing counsel for the defense to argue the constitutionality of the Sedition Act, only whether the accused was guilty under the terms of that act.

In neither case was there any question of the fairness or correctness of the verdicts. Fries had led the rebellion, and Callender's book was by itself evidence of libel. It was Chase's behavior that was being tried.

A further charge stemmed from 1800, when a grand jury in New Castle, Delaware, stated that it had no cases to present. Chase reminded the grand jury that a certain newspaper had printed inflammatory articles and sent it away to examine the paper. The jurors wanted to get to their harvest and resented his instructions. However, when they returned the following day, having found no cause for indictments, Chase dismissed them.

Chase was also charged with making critical comments about the administration of President Jefferson during the time Chase presided as judge in Baltimore. Chase had fortunately written down his statements ahead of time, had read them aloud in Baltimore, and had the written statements handy to reread to the Senate. He said that in retrospect he regretted making those statements, but since the Sedition Act had expired, there was no law against stating his opinion publicly. Hence, he had broken no law.

As each charge against Chase was read, senators voted aloud, guilty or not guilty. On most of the charges he was found not guilty. On at least one, he was found guilty by a simple majority, but not the two-thirds necessary to remove him from his position. Federalists voted not guilty as a bloc. Some Republicans voted not guilty because they disliked John Randolph. Others voted not guilty because they genuinely believed that Randolph had not made a strong enough case, and moreover, that the judiciary should be independent of the executive and legislative branches. Impeachment was therefore only to be used for serious cases of abuse of power or criminal acts.

Jefferson had suffered a political defeat on the eve of his inaugural. Scholars believe that his real target was John Marshall and that Chase was a rehearsal or test case. The result was a change in attitude of the government. The executive and legislative branches pulled back from impeachments, while the judiciary pulled back from expressing partisan feelings and became a more contemplative group.

As for Chase, he continued to serve as a justice until his death in 1811, and Marshall rendered independent decisions for the Supreme Court for three decades.

SOURCES

My main source for the trial itself was Justice William Rehnquist's masterful *Grand Inquests: The Historic Impeachments of Justice Samuel Chase and President Andrew Johnson*, published in 1992 by William Morrow. For a biography of Chase, I read *Stormy Patriot—The Life of Samuel Chase* by James Haw, Francis F. Bierne, Rosamond R. Bierne, and R. Samuel Jett (Baltimore: Maryland Historical Society, 1980). The impeachment is also discussed in Joseph L. Ellis's *American Sphinx* (New York: Alfred A. Knopf, 1996); Dumas Malone's *Jefferson and His Time*, Volume 4, *Jefferson the President, First Term 1801–1805* (Boston: Little, Brown and Company, 1970); Cliff Sloan and David McKean's *The Great Decision—Jefferson, Adams, Marshall and the Battle for the Supreme Court* (New York: Perseus Books, 2009); Joseph Wheelan's *Jefferson's Vendetta* (New York: Carroll & Graf, 2005); Albert Beveridge's *The Life of John Marshall*, Vol. III, Conflict and Construction (Boston: Houghton Mifflin, 1919); Bill Severn's *John Marshall, the Man Who Made the Court Supreme* (New York: David MacKay Company, 1969); Bill Kaufman's *Forgotten Founder, Drunken Prophet—The Life of Luther Martin* (Wilmington, Delaware: ISI Press, 2008); and *Crisis in Freedom: The Alien and Sedition Acts* by John C. Miller (Boston: Little, Brown and Company, 1951).

Andrew Jackson behaved in such a tyrannical manner toward Indians, the British, and the national bank that he was called King Andrew I.
LIBRARY OF CONGRESS

CHAPTER FIVE

Andrew Jackson:
Indian Killer

Andrew Jackson was a man of contradictions: a military hero, popular president, loyal friend, supporter of the "common man." Yet he was a wealthy planter who owned slaves and a rowdy who dueled and allowed his followers to damage the White House. But his treatment of the Cherokee and other Indian tribes has earned him the most criticism. Here he went beyond being a jerk to being guilty of cruelty.

Jackson, the revered American president, was a vengeful man, killing his enemies without mercy.

He might have had reasons for his hatred of certain groups, but as president he needed to let go of his grudges and represent all Americans. He hated the British for the way they had treated his family during the Revolutionary War. He hated Indians because he saw his fellow landowners killed by Indians who had sided with the British. He blamed gossip for his wife's death, and this led him to disrupt his Cabinet because of gossip about a much less worthy woman. He wasted a lot of his time and popularity fighting the Second Bank of the United States, in the end hurting the very people he claimed to help.

Jackson's parents emigrated from Ireland and settled on a small farm in the Waxhaw settlement on the North Carolina-South Carolina border. His father died shortly before young Andrew's birth on March 15, 1767. His mother was left with three small boys to support and had no recourse but to move in with relatives.

During the Revolutionary War the oldest Jackson son, Hugh, died following the Battle of Stono Ferry. Andrew, his mother, and his brother were taken captive by British troops under the direction of the hated Banastre Tarleton. When Andrew was ordered to clean a soldier's boots, he refused, and the soldier slashed at him with his sword. Andrew threw up his hand to defend himself and was cut on the hand and face, the first of many injuries he would sustain throughout his life. His brother died of smallpox, as did his mother, who was caring for prisoners of war being kept on ships in Charleston harbor.

At fourteen Andrew was an orphan, a tall, lanky young man with a violent temper and only a skimpy education. He drifted from place to place, working various jobs, fighting and drinking, until finally deciding to study law. He was certified to practice law in 1787, at the age of twenty, and set off west of the Allegheny Mountains into what is now Tennessee, where he thought there were opportunities for a young lawyer.

In 1788 he arrived in Nashville and went to board with the Donelson family. Here he fell in love with their daughter Rachel, who was unfortunately married to Lewis Robards. To staunch the gossip about them, Andrew took other lodgings, and Robards demanded that Rachel return to him. The marriage was stormy, however, and eventually Rachel could stand the abuse no longer and ran away. Andrew accompanied her to Natchez, and then returned to Nashville.

In 1791 Andrew heard that Robards had divorced Rachel. He went to Natchez, where he married her. They returned to Nash-ville and lived happily for two years. Then word came that in 1791 Robards had only been granted permission to seek a divorce. The actual divorce was not granted until September 1793. Andrew and Rachel had another marriage ceremony performed, but for the rest of their lives together, they would be accused of adultery.

Jackson was appointed public prosecutor in Nashville and in addition had a thriving law practice. Marrying Rachel had been financially a good idea too, as the Donelsons were a prominent family, and Rachel inherited land and slaves. Andrew began buy-ing up land grants, as most settlers did. Sometimes the Indians gave individual titles, but more often blocks of land would be transferred from the Indians to the U.S. government, which would then sell it—or in some cases, give it as deferred payment to soldiers who had fought in the Revolutionary War.

In 1783 North Carolina had passed the Land Grab Act, which permitted citizens to claim Indian land in Tennessee. In one year, over two million acres were claimed. The Indians fought back, killing a settler about every ten days, using weapons furnished by the Spanish, who wanted to stem the tide of American settlers moving west.

The Founding Fathers had thought of Indians as "noble savages," who would eventually be Christianized and assume white people's ways so that they could be assimilated into American society. Ironically, one of the tribes that suffered most, the Cherokee, had become most like white Americans. They had an alphabet, educated their children, had ceased roaming, and built flourishing farms. Therein was the problem. Whites coveted their productive farmland.

In the Treaty of Holston in 1791 the U.S. government paid $5,000 "in suitable goods" to the Cherokee for land illegally seized. New boundaries were drawn, and whites were forbidden to cross into Cherokee territory, but many ignored the treaty. President Washington appointed William Blount governor of the vast territory that included all the area south of the Ohio River to the Mississippi, with jurisdiction over the Cherokee, Creeks, Choctaws, and Chickasaws. He was also elected to the U.S. Senate when Tennessee became a state, but became involved in land speculation and in addition planned a conspiracy with the British, asking their support in taking Florida from Spain. He was impeached, and Andrew Jackson, already Tennessee's first congressman, was elected to the Senate to replace him. But Andrew felt out of place in the Senate and resigned after only one year.

Jackson became a judge in Tennessee, handling many Indian cases. Due to biased juries, the Indians seldom got a fair trial.

President Thomas Jefferson urged shopkeepers on the frontier to keep Indians in debt so that they would be forced to cede land. The suggestion worked, as the Indians sometimes failed to understand the price of the goods and were often given shoddy goods at inflated prices. From 1791 to 1819 the Cherokee signed twenty-five treaties with the federal government, ceding land to cancel debts.

Jackson thought of the Indians as children. When speaking with them he called the president the "father of his red children." He tried to turn one tribe against the other in warfare, but he could also be harsh with whites who broke treaties by taking land. They were troublemakers who put other settlers' lives in danger, he thought, but he had little power to stop the incursions.

Besides being a judge, Jackson was also a member of the Tennessee militia, achieving the rank of general not by experience but because his militiamen voted for him.

In 1806 Jackson fought a duel that almost cost him his life. He quarreled with his neighbor, Charles Dickinson, over a bet on a horse race. The matter could have been settled amicably, but Dickinson made the mistake of bringing up Rachel's "adultery." Jackson challenged him, and the two met later with their seconds. Paces were stepped off, the men turned, and Dickinson fired, hitting Jackson in the chest. Jackson didn't fall but slowly raised his pistol and fired, killing Dickinson. Jackson walked away bleeding. Several ribs had been broken, and a bullet was lodged close to his heart.

On another occasion Jackson was asked to be the second to a young man in a duel against Jesse Benton, brother of Senator Thomas Hart Benton, and reluctantly agreed. Jesse Benton was shot in the buttocks, and a quarrel broke out between the Bentons and Jackson. They attacked him in a bar several months later. Jesse Benton shot Jackson, shattering his shoulder, and a second shot embedded itself in his right arm. This wound would also trouble him for years.

When the War of 1812 began, Jackson was commissioned a major general in the United States Volunteer Army, with orders to go to New Orleans. On the way, the order was rescinded, and Jackson himself paid for food and supplies for his troops on their return to Tennessee.

In August 1813, Creek Indians attacked Fort Mims in present-day Alabama, killing over 250 whites, friendly Indians, and mixed Indian-whites. A few escaped to tell of the barbarity. Jackson was ordered to subdue the Creek Indians in Alabama, who were allied with British troops. He received the cooperation of friendly Creeks and Cherokee by promising them the protection of the U.S. government. Indians and militia surrounded Tallushatchee, the village of the hostile Red Sticks, and attacked. Warriors were killed, cabins burned, and women and children taken prisoner. Contrary to the usual practice of killing male children who would grow up to be warriors, Jackson saved a child, Lyncoya. He said that he felt a kinship with the orphaned child, for he had also been orphaned. Jackson sent Lyncoya to The Hermitage, his home in Tennessee, where Rachel cared for the child. The Jacksons, who had no children of their own, treated him as their son.

Jackson led troops to attack at Talladega, killing hundreds of Indians. Jackson's unflinching courage in battle and in facing down deserters when supplies were running low earned him the nickname "Old Hickory" from his men, as hickory was the hardest wood they knew.

While Jackson was attempting to make peace with two other small tribes, General James White attacked the villages, slaughtering Indians and burning their homes. Jackson got the blame for "tricking" the friendly Indians.

Enlistments were up for many of the militia, and Jackson sent them back to Tennessee on January 14. That same day, new recruits arrived, and the general marched his troops to Horseshoe Bend, where he wiped out the settlement, killing approximately 850 Red Sticks (Creeks). Jackson lost twenty-six Americans, eighteen Cherokee, and five friendly Creeks.

Jackson demanded that the government "extinguish" all Cherokee land titles in Tennessee and that the Creeks be moved westward so that a strip of land separated them from the Indians in Spanish Florida. He was made a brigadier general and put in charge of Tennessee, Louisiana, the Mississippi Territory, and the Creek nation, so that he was in a position to carry out the edicts.

The War of 1812 was going badly for America. The British won battles in the Great Lakes and even burned Washington, D.C. Then on January 8, 1815, Jackson dealt a stunning defeat to the British General Edward Pakenham. With a volunteer army made up of frontier farmers, Indians, and even pirates, on a mist-shrouded field near New Orleans, Jackson drove back the proud army of Redcoats. Jackson lost a dozen men, while the British dead numbered 251 and their total casualties were 2,000, which included those injured, missing, and captured. It was an unnecessary battle, since both sides had decided in Europe to sign a treaty, but word had not arrived in America. The victory signaled to the world that America could defend itself, and it established a new American champion, Andrew Jackson.

Jackson would be rewarded. He asked that a road be built from New Orleans to Nashville, that forts be built along the southern border with Spanish Florida, and that the Indians be moved west-ward out of the United States into unsettled territory. He gave no thought to the fact that other Indian tribes inhabited the western lands. He commanded half the troops in the United States and was also Indian commissioner. What he wanted would be done.

The Cherokee, meanwhile, went to Washington, D.C., to ask for guaranteed title to their land and payment for damages done by Tennessee militia. They were promised $25,000. Jackson told the Indians they should sell their land and use the money to educate their children, build farms, and buy slaves—but out west. Some Cherokee protested that if they were ever to become "civilized" they must live near whites.

Meanwhile, in Florida the Seminoles, protected by the Span-ish, were attacking farms across the border in Georgia and harbor-ing runaway slaves. A fort was attacked on the border, Americans were killed, and a woman was taken prisoner. Jackson wrote to John C. Calhoun, President James Monroe's secretary of war, ask-ing permission to fight the Seminoles. Calhoun, who had been one of the "War Hawks" who pushed President James Madison into war in 1812, gave general permission, commanding him to "put down the Seminole problem," though he later denied it. Jackson decided to seize all of Florida, which was an act of war against Spain, and he called for volunteers to fight in Florida without asking permission of Congress.

Jackson took over Spanish Florida, sent the commandant of Fort St. Marks and his family to Pensacola, and raised the American flag over the fort. He executed two British citizens as spies, and a British captain managed to escape to Cuba. Jackson trumped up Spanish demands and though they were met, he took Pensacola anyway and installed an American governor there. He wrote to President Monroe that with a flotilla he could take Cuba. Fortunately no flotilla arrived.

His campaign was not a total success. Militia from Georgia and Alabama marched into the territory, killing friendly Indians whom Jackson had promised to protect and burning their villages.

Secretary of State John Quincy Adams negotiated a treaty with the Spanish in 1819 to cede Florida to the United States for $5 million. The Spanish also agreed to relinquish their claims to the Oregon Territory. In the House of Representatives, Henry Clay tried to have Jackson censured for his high-handed actions.

Jackson spent a few years at home with Rachel before a "boomlet" began to support him for president. In the election of 1824, Jackson won the most votes—43 percent—but not a majority. John Quincy Adams was second, Henry Clay third. The election thus went to the House of Representatives with each state having one vote. Clay persuaded enough electors to vote for Adams that Adams was elected president. Soon after, he named Clay to be secretary of state. Jackson's followers cried that the election had been a "corrupt bargain" and set out to elect their man in 1828.

They succeeded, thanks to slogans, barbecues, and parades, many of them led by people carrying hickory sticks. It was the first such campaign. Besides the showiness, however, it was an ugly campaign. Both Rachel and Andrew were defamed. Newspapers called him vile names and brought up the old charge of adultery against her.

When the votes were counted, Jackson was elected president and John Calhoun of South Carolina was elected vice president. This pairing would break up over a woman, but not Rachel this time. Rachel Jackson died in December 1828, knowing that her husband had been elected president but before his inaugural. She apparently died of a heart attack, which Jackson believed had been brought on by the stress of the slurs and name-calling.

Jackson's inaugural was a mob scene. The "common people" claimed him as their own. He was the first president from the west and a military man as George Washington had been—unlike the intervening presidents: Adams, Jefferson, Madison, and Monroe. The crowd overran the White House, where a small party had been planned, and ran rampant. They scarred floors with muddy hob-nailed boots, broke punch bowls, got into food fights, and tore the damask upholstery of White House furniture. Eventually Jackson himself slipped out, and the waiters took the punch bowls onto the lawn to attract the unruly mob outside.

To get the support of the South in 1828, Jackson had chosen Calhoun as his vice president, unaware that Calhoun had earlier tried to undermine him. The two men split, however, not over Indian policy but because of tariffs and a woman. John Eaton, Jackson's secretary of war, had married Margaret "Peggy" O'Neale Timberlake, a tavern keeper's daughter, very soon after her husband's death. Other Cabinet wives, led by Mrs. Calhoun, scorned her and refused to invite the Eatons to social events. Jackson, remembering Rachel's treatment, showed special favor to the Eatons.

Jackson wanted to get rid of Cabinet members who had shunned Mrs. Eaton, but could find no legal reason for their dismissal. Martin Van Buren, secretary of state, suggested that as a solution he would resign and all other Cabinet members should also resign. Jackson could then nominate new men. The plan worked. Eaton was made governor of Florida, and Van Buren was named minister to Great Britain. The Senate confirmation of Van Buren resulted in a tie. Vice President Calhoun, in his position as president of the Senate, voted no to break the tie, making a political mistake. Van Buren was thus on hand to become Jackson's running mate in 1832 instead of Calhoun, who had also led a movement to nullify the collection of federal tariffs in South Carolina. He resigned before his term was up and was elected to the Senate.

Jackson hated banks because he thought they put power into the hands of rich Eastern men, keeping down the common people from the west. He especially opposed the Second Bank of the United States, which held government deposits and was paying dividends to a few wealthy Americans and even foreigners. He let his displeasure be known, and Nicholas Biddle, president of the bank, decided to push the matter. He asked that the bank be rechartered four years early and spent bank money to elect members of Congress favorable to the bank. This proved Jackson's contention about the bank's power. Jackson had his acting secretary of the treasury withdraw funds from the bank to pay government expenses and deposited revenue in state banks. Biddle then called in loans from branch banks, and those banks thus could make no further loans. A recession resulted. Both Jackson and Biddle got the blame. Eventually, without incoming funds from the government, the Second Bank of the United States shrank. Biddle resigned, and an investigation indicated misuse of funds, possibly fraud.

Jackson's continuing problem was what to do about the Indians. He felt he had four choices, none of them very good. First, all Indians east of the Mississippi could be killed. He and the army had come close with some tribes, and others had died off from disease. Second, the Indians could assimilate into white society, but there was too much racism in America for this to work, he thought. Moreover, the Indians themselves wanted to maintain their way of life and their sovereignty. Third, they could be restricted to certain areas and their lives and property protected by a standing army. Jackson thought this was impossible. The army could not be everywhere all the time. Fourth, they could be removed.

There should be voluntary removals, Jackson stated, but if the Indians did not voluntarily go, then they were subject to the laws of the state they resided in. They would have no more sovereignty as tribes or nations, despite treaties to the contrary, including one signed by George Washington.

Repeated treaties and forced purchases of Indian land had resulted in most of the land east of the Mississippi being owned by whites. One of the early "accomplishments" of Jackson's first administration was the Indian Removal Act of 1830, requiring that all Indians must be moved west of the Mississippi. Indians had gone west and seen the land. They felt it was unsuitable for their way of life—they were used to forests, rich land, and ample rainfall, not the arid, windy plains. They were placated by being given more acres in the West than they surrendered east of the Mississippi.

The Cherokee held out longer than any other tribe. Finally, in a matter of weeks in 1838, the Georgia militia rounded up over 17,000 Cherokee and put them in a stockade until the journey to the Indian Territory (now Oklahoma) could begin. They were taken down the Tennessee River on steamboats, then in crowded boxcars on trains, and finally made their way on foot in what is called "The Trail of Tears." More than 4,000 died on the way, of starvation, sickness, and injuries.

In all, over 60,000 Eastern Indians were moved west of the Mississippi. A few Cherokee hid out in the misty mountains of western North Carolina and eastern Tennessee, and were allowed to remain.

Jackson had gotten his revenge on the bank, the British, and especially the Indians.

SOURCES

Robert V. Remini is a renowned Jacksonian scholar, and I read three of his books on Andrew Jackson: *The Life of Andrew Jack-*

son (New York: Harper & Row, 1988); *Andrew Jackson and His Indian Wars* (New York: Viking, 2001); and *The Revolutionary Age of Andrew Jackson* (New York: Harper & Row, 1976). I also read *The Passions of Andrew Jackson* by Andrew Burstein (New York: Alfred A. Knopf, 2003); *Andrew Jackson: His Contribution to the American Tradition* by Harold C. Sybett (Westport, Conn.: Greenwood Press, 1956); and an oldie, Tom W. Campbell's *Two Fighters and Two Fines: Sketches of the Lives of Matthew Lyon and Andrew Jackson* (Little Rock, Ark.: Pioneer Publishing Company, 1941). John Ehle's *Trail of Tears: The Rise and Fall of the Cherokee Nation* (New York: Random House, 1988) tells the sad story of the Cherokee nation and their forced removal. A brief retelling of the stories of Rachel Donelson Jackson and of Peggy Eaton can be found in Chapter 6, "God Help the Women Who Must Live in Washington," in *Fall From Grace: Sex, Scandal, and Corruption in American Politics from 1702 to the Present* by Shelley Ross (New York: Random House, 1988).

Jackson also appears prominently in biographies of his contemporaries: Roger Taney, Henry Clay, John C. Calhoun, Daniel Webster, Martin Van Buren, John Quincy Adams, and even Aaron Burr—Jackson attended his trial in Richmond, Virginia.

Dan Sickles shortly before he lost his leg at Gettysburg. Undeterred by his handi-cap, he was a military governor of the Carolinas and an ambassador, and had an affair with a deposed queen.
LIBRARY OF CONGRESS

CHAPTER SIX

Dan Sickles:
The Killer Congressman

When Congressman Daniel Edgar Sickles of New York and his lovely young wife, Teresa, arrived in Washington, D.C., in early 1857 for the inaugural of President James Buchanan, life looked promising for them. Dan was a "comer," a friend of the president's, and the couple could entertain and be entertained in lavish Washington style. No one could have predicted that within two years both would be disgraced, she for adultery, he for murder.

Dan had been a headstrong child but such a charmer that no matter how outrageously he acted, he was forgiven and taken back into others' good graces. When he didn't like the school his parents sent him to, he ran away and became a printer. His parents persuaded Dan to return home to New York and work on a farm his father had just bought.

After a year Dan had had enough and ran away again, working as a printer first in Trenton and then in Philadelphia. He agreed to return to New York on condition that he be allowed to study with Lorenzo da Ponte, a classics professor. Living in the da Ponte home were Italian musician Antonio Bagioli, his wife, and their baby daughter, Teresa. Here Dan learned languages and began taking classes at the University of the City of New York (later New York University).

After da Ponte's death, Dan dropped out of college and studied law in the office of Benjamin Butler, who had been a law partner of President Martin Van Buren. This gave Dan an entrée into politics.

Soon young Dan was in with the Tammany Hall crowd, which dominated New York City politics, and was elected to city and state offices. His law practice flourished, and he was named corporation counsel for the City of New York. One accomplishment was persuading New Yorkers to turn a rough, boulder-strewn swamp into Central Park. Never able to manage money, he was sued several times for debt, fraud, and mishandling funds. He also destroyed several bags of mail that held political flyers for a friend's opponent, but activities like these were "business as usual" in nineteenth-century New York.

Dan stepped over the accepted line when he took his mistress, a known prostitute, to tour the state government offices in Albany. He also took her to London when he went as secretary and assistant to James Buchanan, newly appointed minister to England. Dan was committing adultery, as by this time he had married Teresa.

At the time of their marriage, Teresa was sixteen, Dan thirty-two. Both her parents and his disapproved of the marriage, but Dan had probably seduced the lovely, dark-haired Teresa. They had a civil ceremony in August 1852, followed in March 1853 by a Catholic service, at which Teresa was noticeably pregnant. Teresa gave birth to their daughter Laura and stayed behind in America until the baby was old enough to travel while Dan went to England.

Buchanan, who was unmarried, had as his hostess his niece Harriet Lane. Both Buchanan and Harriet became fond of Teresa, whose facility with foreign languages was an asset to the American minister. Buchanan saw to it that Teresa was introduced to Queen Victoria, and rumors spread that he was a bit too fond of eighteen-year-old Mrs. Sickles.

In 1856, Buchanan, a Democrat, ran for U.S. president, and Dan campaigned for him all over New York State, leaving Teresa and Laura in their new home in Bloomingdale, about seven miles from downtown Manhattan. The campaigning paid off. Buchanan was elected president that November, and Dan was elected to Congress from the Third District.

In Washington for the inaugural of Buchanan, Dan and Teresa stayed at the home of Jonah Hoover, marshal of the District of

Columbia. Teresa then returned to New York while Dan remained in Washington, though the session of Congress would not begin until December. Dan and Philip Barton Key, son of the composer Francis Scott Key, played whist at Hoover's and later at the National Hotel. They had met four years earlier at the inaugural of President Franklin Pierce. The two men became friends, and Dan used his influence to make sure that Barton, as he was called, kept his position as district attorney for the District of Columbia, a post he'd been appointed to by Pierce.

While Dan was away in New York, he asked Key to settle the legal matters in purchasing a house Dan wanted, the Stockton mansion on Lafayette Park, near the White House. It was to become very familiar to Key.

Dan, Teresa, and Laura moved into the fashionable residence and joined the gala society of Washington. They had chosen a prestigious area. Their neighbors included Speaker of the House James Orr, Senator John Slidell, and wealthy art collector W. W. Corcoran.

Dan and Teresa attended dinners and parties at the White House and gave elaborate dinners of their own on Thursday evenings. On Tuesdays Teresa made her social rounds, calling briefly on other hostesses and partaking of refreshments. Sometimes Philip Barton Key happened to be attending at the same time. Key was widowed, with four children, and was considered one of the most eligible men in Washington. He was available to escort women to dances or accompany them on morning horseback rides. He escorted a number of young ladies, but gradually the others were dropped and he was frequently seen with Teresa.

Dan often worked late at the Capitol or made out-of-town trips, sometimes to see other women, and he didn't object to having young men escort Teresa to social functions. She was described as having a soft, vulnerable air, and yet it was combined with a sultry beauty. Several young men fell in love with her, and like other belles of her time, she flirted. One frequent escort was Dan's sophisticated New York friend, Henry Wickoff, who had taken her to the pier to see her husband off to England in 1853. Dan approved of Wickoff's spending time with Teresa. But more and more, her attention focused on Key, and he began to call on her at the mansion when Dan was away.

Tongues wagged. It was one thing for a man to frequent prostitutes or to have a long-standing affair, but his wife was to be above reproach. Dan conducted his affairs with a certain amount of discretion, and away from Washington. Teresa did not. She probably suspected that her husband had other women, but she dared not confront him and ask for a divorce. What other life was there for her? She tried hard to please Dan and to be a good congressional wife, shopping, supervising their three servants, spending time with Laura, and planning social activities.

One of the young men smitten with Teresa told Dan she was having an affair with Key, but he had no proof, and Key forced him to retract his story. There was indeed no sexual affair at that time. Then one night Teresa and Key made love on the sofa in the parlor of the Sickles home. After that, there was no turning back.

The servants quickly caught on to Key's signal: He would stand outside in the street and wave his handkerchief, then walk away. Teresa would summon the coachman to take her on an outing, and a few blocks from Lafayette Park, the carriage would stop for Key. The servants called the arrangement "Disgrace coming for Disgust."

When the session of Congress ended in June 1858, the Sickles family returned to their home in Bloomingdale. Barton Key visited them twice during the summer. Dan was reelected to Congress, and the family returned to Washington for the session that began in December. Again Dan was hard at work, and Teresa and Barton were together.

For more privacy, Key rented a small, two-story brick house at 383 Fifteenth Street, where he and Teresa could be together, but they were indiscreet. Neighbors soon became used to seeing them arrive separately, spend an hour together, and depart separately or together. The signal that the other was waiting was a ribbon hanging from an upper window. Teresa sometimes came veiled, as was the custom for a rendezvous, but she sometimes lifted her veil before she entered the house. At any rate, the neighbors noticed her clothing and could accurately describe it.

The lovers were living in a fool's paradise, heedless of the consequences. It came to a tragic end when someone sent Dan an anonymous letter, signed "R.P.G.," telling him about the secret meetings. The following day Dan placed an ad in the newspaper asking R.P.G. to identify himself but received no answer. Dan never found out who R.P.G. was but decided to follow up on the accusations. He went to the house on Fifteenth Street and talked with neighbors, who confirmed the meetings.

That night, February 26, 1859, Dan confronted Teresa in her bedroom and called a guest to witness that his wife was writing her confession. Although Dan probably dictated what she was to write, Teresa admitted to the affair and wrote what was at that time a lurid account of undressing and waiting for Key to arrive, then "doing what a fallen woman would do." She signed it "Teresa Bagioli," not "Sickles."

The next morning Dan sent for his friend, Samuel Butterworth, and showed him the letter. Butterworth advised sending Teresa to her mother in New York. Dan claimed that the affair was widely known and must be settled as a "matter of honor." While the men talked in the library, Key appeared in front of the house several times, waving his handkerchief, and each time he went away. In the early afternoon Dan and Butterworth went in search of Key. Dan was armed with two derringers and a revolver.

Soon Key appeared, and Butterworth spoke to him so that Key turned toward Dan Sickles. Dan called out, "You scoundrel! You have dishonored my home and you must die!" He shot, but the bullet only grazed Key. The two men grappled and broke apart. Dan fired again, hitting Key in the groin. Key threw his opera glass at Dan and cried, "Don't murder me!" He fell against a tree and slid to the ground. Dan shot again, piercing Key's chest, then brought the gun up to Key's face and pulled the trigger. The gun misfired, but it didn't matter. Key was dying. Twelve witnesses had seen the murder, and Butterworth, who might have stopped Dan, did nothing.

There was blame enough to go around that day. Key's body was taken to the nearby Clubhouse, and by the time the coroner arrived, rings had been taken off the victim's hands and items were removed from his pockets. It was clear to all that he had not been armed.

One witness, a page, ran to tell President Buchanan of the murder. Buchanan, not realizing there were other witnesses, lied to the boy and told him he would be arrested and should leave Washington. He gave the page money to make the journey, and the young man left the capital for good. Butterworth also left Washington for New York and was never subpoenaed or questioned.

Dan was apparently a good actor. He seemed calm to his friends immediately after the shooting, then cried in "paroxysms of grief" when told that he should turn himself in, but was calm again when he told Teresa, "I have killed him."

After an autopsy conducted in Key's home, a funeral service was held, and his body was taken by train to Baltimore, where he was buried next to his late wife, Ellen.

Dan was arrested and first placed in an ordinary "vermin-infested" cell, then transferred to the jailer's office. Newspapers all over the East took up the case. Most blamed Key for having seduced a "frail" woman and declared that he deserved being shot. The writers felt that Dan was justified in defending his honor, and Teresa was scorned.

Dan's father came to visit, and Dan asked that seven-year-old Laura be brought to the jail to see him. Friends offered to bail him out, but he refused and asked for a speedy trial. The grand jury indicted him, and his trial was set for April 4, only thirty-six days after the murder.

Dan's lawyers included noted criminal attorney James T. Brady and Edwin M. Stanton—Buchanan's attorney general and later secretary of war in Lincoln's Cabinet—as well as four other lawyers. Despite the witnesses and evidence, they had their client plead not guilty.

The prosecutor was Robert Ould, Barton Key's assistant, a man unused to criminal prosecutions of this magnitude.

The defense presented Dan as the wronged husband driven insane by the knowledge of his wife's perfidy. He was depicted as acting under an "irresistible impulse," and for the very first time the plea of "temporary insanity" was used. It worked. Dan was acquitted, even though his "temporary" insanity had lasted long enough for him to force a confession from his wife, send for friends and discuss the matter with them, then seek out the victim.

He was a jerk and a murderer, but he was free. Most Washingtonians and New Yorkers thought the verdict was the right one. A man must avenge the despoliation of his wife.

Dan Sickles plotted the murder of his wife's lover and shot him before twenty witnesses, yet was acquitted.
GOOGLEIMAGES

Public support turned against him when word got out that Dan had forgiven Teresa and would take her back—that indeed they had written letters to each other the whole time he was in jail. Friends, enemies, and the general public demanded to know why— if he was going to forgive Teresa—he had not forgiven Barton Key instead of killing him? Dan found himself ostracized in Congress. Teresa went to live in the Bloomingdale mansion, secluded.

Dan again tried to do something popular, by arranging for Washington's birthday to be celebrated as a national holiday. His career, however, was not revived until the coming of the Civil War.

Soon after Lincoln was elected, Southern states seceded and Dan's Southern neighbors and fellow congressmen left Washington. South Carolina seized Fort Moultrie and demanded that Fort Sumter be evacuated. President Buchanan couldn't decide what to do, and Attorney General Stanton asked Dan to persuade the president to hold on to the fort. Dan thought the South had a right to secede but not to act violently toward the Union. He knew the way President Buchanan's mind worked and practiced an old Tammany Hall subterfuge. He took the train north and at each major city he asked the mayor and influential citizens to send the president telegrams praising him for holding fast and not giving in to the South. It worked.

When war began, Dan Sickles proposed to President Lincoln that he could raise a regiment, promising to pay for it himself. The New York governor commanded him to raise a brigade, which Sickles did, calling it the Excelsior Brigade, and Sickles became a brigadier general. But where would thousands of troops stay? Boarding them in the city was expensive, and out on Long Island there were no amenities. None of the men, including Sickles himself, had any military training. When the troops became an expensive burden, Dan's enemies demanded that the brigade be disbanded. Dan signed notes for payment, assuming that the federal government would reimburse him, and took his troops South. At the end of the war some of the bills still had not been paid.

Sickles was a quick learner and put his troops to good use in the Peninsula Campaign, at Fredericksburg and at Chancellorsville, under several commanders. The Union army made a series of blunders under commanders who were either too timid to attack or too arrogant to learn from their mistakes.

Ever the adventurer, Sickles went up in a hot air observation balloon over the Potomac to observe Confederate troops.

Despite losses in numbers, Sickles still had a substantial force to fight at Gettysburg. Told by General George Meade to stay back in a glen, Sickles led his forces into what was referred to as The Peach Orchard, right in the forefront of Confederate General

James Longstreet's attack. Sickles later claimed that his action saved the day for the Union, while Meade said that Sickles's disobedience cost unnecessary lives.

Sickles was sitting on his horse on the battlefield when a cannonball tore into his lower leg. He was taken to the field hospital where the leg was amputated at mid-thigh. Most amputated limbs were tossed outside to be buried, but Sickles insisted on keeping his leg, preserved in formaldehyde, which he sent to the Army Medical Museum in Washington. It was jokingly referred to as "Sickles' Pickle." For the rest of his life, Sickles visited his leg at regular intervals.

Out of active service, he was fitted with an artificial leg, but he preferred the obvious sign of his loss, crutches and a pinned-up trouser leg.

President Lincoln sent Sickles on a mission to check over the newly liberated territory: west to Tennessee, south to Arkansas and New Orleans, then back up the coast. On this journey he met and came to like Andrew Johnson, who became Lincoln's running mate in 1864. Sickles abandoned the Democrats to vote for Lincoln and Johnson.

He was sent on another mission, this time to Colombia and Panama, to determine if either place would be suitable for resettlement of the freed slaves. He considered the possibility of building a canal across Panama but was unable to secure any financial backers, not surprising given his long history of mismanagement of money. He was away at the time Lincoln was assassinated.

President Johnson appointed Sickles to be the military governor first of South Carolina and then of both Carolinas, with an army of 7,000 troops under his command. Dan became unpopular when he established martial law, had some Confederates arrested, and ignored a summons to federal court. Johnson removed him.

In 1867 Teresa died, and at her funeral the praise was mostly for Dan, the widower, rather than for the departed.

What was to be done with a popular, headstrong general? He had supported the Republican Ulysses Grant for president, and in return Grant made Dan a full general and appointed him minister to Spain. Still a womanizer and an adventurer, Dan had an affair with the deposed Queen Isabella II, married a young noblewoman, Caroline Creagh, and helped overthrow an unpopular government. He also managed to find time to return to America and oust the robber baron Jay Gould from control of the Erie Railroad, earning Sickles the largest legal fee of his career and inadvertently adding to Gould's fortune when the price of the railroad's stock rose dramatically after Gould's ouster.

All along, Dan was pushing for Spain to sell Cuba to the United States. A rebellion against Spain was taking place on the island, and Americans were helping the rebels. Then an American ship, *The Virginius*, was seized and fifty-two of her crew and passengers were lined up and shot. Sickles pushed for war with Spain, but President Grant and his secretary of state, Hamilton Fish, met in Washington with the Spanish ambassador and negotiated a satisfactory end to the matter. Sickles thought they had shown weakness and leaked news of the situation to the New York press. He was removed from his post.

Sickles, his wife, Caroline, and daughter Laura moved to Paris. Here he did some "service" for the French government that earned him the Legion of Honor, and here his wife bore him a daughter, Eda, and a son, George Stanton. In 1880 Sickles decided to return to America and enter politics again, but Caroline refused to move. He left without her.

It was time for another election, and Sickles wanted Grant to have a third term, but the president failed to get enough votes for the nomination, and James A. Garfield became president instead.

Sickles was a man without a job. He worked on various commissions and met with groups of Civil War veterans. Finally in 1893 he was again elected to Congress, where he formed a friendship with his former enemy, James Longstreet. Together the two managed to have Congress buy the Gettysburg battlefield and turn it into a national historical park.

When Sickles's father, George, died, Dan inherited $5 million, a huge fortune for the time. He was solvent for a while, but frittered his money away in bad investments and generous gifts for anyone who caught his fancy. He lived to see the Spanish American War, by which America got control of Cuba, and to have a reconciliation with his children. His wife was with him when he died following a stroke in 1914.

Daniel Sickles's contemporaries once thought he was headed for the presidency, a goal he might have achieved had he not killed Philip Barton Key.

What kind of president would Sickles have been? America was spared by his stupid act of murder.

Sources

I first encountered Daniel Sickles in Michael Farquhar's *A Treasury of Great American Scandals* (New York: Penguin Books, 2003) and soon realized that Sickles richly deserved the term "jerk." I ran across him again in Shelley Ross's *Fall from Grace: Sex, Scandal and Corruption in American Politics from 1702 to the Present* (New York: Ballantine Books, 1988). I read *The Congressman Who Got Away with Murder*, by Nat Brandt (Syracuse, N.Y.: Syracuse University Press, 1991), which gave a detailed account of the murder, the trial, the developing affair between Teresa Sickles and Barton Key, and life in Washington, D.C., in the 1850s. Both *American Scoundrel: The Life of the Notorious Civil War General Dan Sickles* by Thomas Keneally (New York: Doubleday, 2002) and *Sickles the Incredible* by W. A. Swanberg (Gettysburg, Pa.: Stan Clark Military Books, 1956) gave more information about the military and diplomatic career of Sickles after the murder—if indeed Sickles could ever have been considered "diplomatic." Swanberg's book had detailed information about Sickles's military actions in the Virginia campaigns of the Civil War and at Gettysburg, and contained useful and interesting photos.

A friend, Bill Holmes, sent me the Web link from the History Channel that had a short feature on Sickles, including the history of his amputated leg.

CHAPTER SEVEN

Brooks and Sumner:
One Damn Fool Beats Another

On May 20, 1856, Senator Charles Sumner finally concluded his two-day inflammatory speech, "The Crime against Kansas," in which he had insulted three colleagues. One of them, Stephen A. Douglas of Illinois, declared, "That damn fool will get himself killed by some other fool."

Douglas was not alone in his antagonism toward Sumner. Sumner had a long history of alienating people. His enemies and even some of his friends had for years expected him to get his comeuppance. Sumner was so opinionated that if someone disagreed with him even partially, he proclaimed that person totally wrong, foolish, and deranged.

Charles considered his a deprived childhood. His mother worked as a seamstress to help support the family of nine children. Charles attended public school, but managed to teach himself Latin. Impressed, his father sent him to the Latin school but

Preston Brooks canes Charles Sumner: "One damn fool beats another."
GOOGLEIMAGES

warned Charles that he couldn't afford college. The family fortunes changed when Charles's father was made sheriff of Essex County, Massachusetts, and Charles was sent to Harvard. After graduation, he spent an idle year at home, planning a literary career. His father urged him to attend Harvard Law School.

Here Charles found structure, a way to combine his love of Greek and Latin literature with law, and friends and mentors who would guide his life. The most important mentor was Joseph Story, associate justice of the Supreme Court. So impressed was Story with Sumner that when he had legal duties in Washington, he had Charles lecture in his place. There would someday be a professorship for him, Story predicted. Sumner's friends thought that he needed to "overcome his shyness and diffidence, and his willingness to be exploited by others so that he might make a name for himself." He would succeed at that effort beyond their wildest expectations.

Charles borrowed money from his friends and—armed with introductions to lawyers, judges, writers, and high-born Europeans—he set off in 1837 for two remarkable years abroad. He studied languages and moved among high society, meeting nobility and even having a seat at Queen Victoria's coronation.

On his return to America, he moved into his then-widowed mother's home and helped support the family. He had a successful law practice, thanks in part to the clients sent to him by Story and Simon Greenleaf. However, he felt adrift because of the marriages of all his friends. They tried to interest him in several women, to no avail. Sumner could never stand rejection, which he would have risked if he proposed to a woman.

He took on a heavy load of editing chancery reports for publication, for a $2,000 fee, but his health failed and he was bedridden. This was to be a pattern for the rest of his life: Stress and high expectations brought on "nervous collapse."

Impressed with Horace Mann's educational reforms, Sumner started raising money for Mann to build an experimental school. Sumner borrowed the necessary $5,000 so the school could be quickly built, but contributions from others dried up and he was left in debt.

In 1845, he was asked to deliver a speech for the Fourth of July in Boston, and he gave a scathing denunciation of the war with Mexico, the annexation of Texas—which he thought was just another way to increase slave territory—and of all war and the military. In later speeches and letters, he called his former class-mate, Congressman Robert Winthrop, a "Pontius Pilate," and com-pared the South to the Barbary pirates. He alienated many of his Whig friends but attracted the attention of John Quincy Adams and other abolitionists. From then on, he campaigned for repeal of the Fugitive Slave Act. Though it was law and constitutional, Sumner said arrogantly that he would uphold the Constitution as he understood it and not as other men understood it.

Perhaps because of his outspokenness and his attitude toward the Constitution, he was passed over for a teaching job at Har-vard Law School. Sumner was bitterly disappointed. He joined the Free-Soil Party, but when he realized that the party had little influence, he became a Democrat.

When Senator Daniel Webster of Massachusetts was named secretary of state, Congressman Winthrop was named senator by the Massachusetts legislature. At the time senators were selected by the legislatures of each state, while congressmen were elected by popular vote. Sumner ran for Winthrop's seat in the House of Representatives but received fewer than five hundred votes.

The Free-Soilers and the Democrats joined forces in 1850, in a move the Whigs called corrupt. The Free-Soilers wanted to reform the state government and were quite willing to let Sumner have the national stage. He ran for the Senate, which the Free-Soilers saw as "of little importance." The Whigs in the legislature stalled, unwilling to choose a senator until after the next fall's election, when they planned to again take control of the state. Sumner's nomination dragged on for two months. He was chosen on the twenty-first ballot, but on two of those ballots more votes were cast than there were members of the legislature. Finally each man was required to vote with a sealed envelope, and on the twenty-sixth ballot, Sumner became a U.S. senator.

When he arrived in Washington, Senator Thomas Hart Benton told him he had arrived on the national scene too late, as "all the great issues are done." Despite his hatred of slavery, Sumner found that he liked many of the Southern senators, especially Andrew Pickens Butler, who had the seat next to Sumner's. Butler often asked Sumner to verify quotations and correct usage in his speeches. Sumner considered Stephen Douglas a "vulgar upstart."

Sumner's first speech was in favor of using government funds for a railroad in Iowa. He claimed it was "the most important speech for the west uttered in Congress for ten years." He wrote out his speech beforehand and memorized it, never feeling comfortable in debate or extemporaneous speaking, and he used the occasion to show off his rhetoric. His speeches always included reams of statistics, exaggeration, and quotations from Latin and from English literature, but never a joke. "You might as well look for a joke in the Book of Revelation," he said of his speeches.

The abolitionists in Massachusetts threatened that he would be dead at the next election if he did not bring up the Fugitive Slave Act and speak against it. He tried, proposing a resolution to repeal the act. Douglas, along with Butler and other Southerners, refused him permission to speak, because the issue of slavery would add to the growing split between North and South.

Then, in the closing days of the Senate session, a bill was presented to pay the expenses of running the government, including administering the Fugitive Slave Act. Sumner seized the opportunity, proposing that no appropriations be used to pay for enforcing the act. He went on speaking for nearly four hours. Afterward, although various members said it was an impressive speech, it changed no minds.

Back in Massachusetts, the Whigs took control again, and Edward Everett was elected the state's second senator. Sumner had alienated too many of his fellow senators and quarreled with

Everett, so he was kept off important committees, while Everett was appointed to them.

In the 1853 session of Congress, Douglas proposed that the question of slavery in the Kansas and Nebraska territories should be voted on by the residents of those territories. Sumner asked for five days' delay so that he could study the bill. Douglas agreed. That same afternoon the Washington papers carried an article Sumner had prepared, calling Douglas's plan anti-immigrant and anti-Christian, among other charges, and slandering Douglas himself. Douglas was rightly angry at the hypocrisy.

After the act passed, Sumner said he would not enforce it. There were calls for him to be expelled from the Senate, inasmuch as he had sworn to uphold the Constitution and the laws of the United States. He was at the very least guilty of perjury for swearing falsely.

William Seward, a moderate anti-slavery senator, urged Sumner to hold his tongue and not do or say anything further to anger Douglas. For a short time, he followed Seward's advice. Then he alienated Seward, one of his last friends. Seward asked him to support a subsidy for a New York steamship company, in what would now be called an "earmark." Sumner said it was uneconomical. Seward said it was important to his reelection, to which Sumner retorted that he did not come to the Senate to look out for anyone else's political future.

Civil war had broken out in Kansas over the issue of slavery, with each side armed but claiming it was not. Rioting and attacks happened regularly.

Sumner saw that the rise in Massachusetts of the Know-Nothing Party, which was both anti-slavery and anti-immigrant, threatened his reelection. He decided to issue a volume of his collected speeches, and his publishers requested a sensational speech to end the book with.

Sumner prepared a speech called "The Crime against Kansas," which he began giving on May 19, 1856. The entire speech ran for 112 printed pages and was generally appropriate to the topic, though at the end of the third hour he got into personal attacks, calling Senator Butler the Don Quixote of slavery, who had made a vow to an unholy mistress, "polluted to the world, but chaste to him, a harlot." Douglas, he said, was "the squire of slavery, Sancho Panza, ready to do all its humiliating offices."

The following day Sumner was at it again, calling attention to the effects of a stroke Senator Butler had had: "incoherent phrases, discharged the loose expectorations of his speech." "Nor was there any possible deviation from truth which he did not make. . . . But the senator touches nothing which he does not disfigure—with error, sometimes of principle, sometimes of fact. He cannot ope his mouth, but there flies out a blunder."

Sumner next criticized the entire state of South Carolina: "Were the whole history of South Carolina blotted out . . . civilization might lose—I do not say how little, but surely less than it has already gained by the example of Kansas." He turned to Senator James Mason, "who represents that other Virginia, from which Washington and Jefferson now avert their faces."

Senator Lewis Cass of Michigan called the speech "the most un-American and unpatriotic that ever grated on the ears of the members of this high body." Douglas noted that Sumner had rehashed old arguments and added nothing but personal attacks. Mason said that it was necessary in government for him to treat someone as an equal whom he would shun and despise in other circumstances.

Sumner stated that he would let Douglas have the last word, except that "no . . . man can be allowed . . . to switch out from his tongue the perpetual stench of offensive personality. The noisome, squat and nameless animal, to which I now refer, is not the proper model for an American senator. Will the senator from Illinois take notice?"

"I will," Douglas answered, "and therefore will not imitate you, sir."

As the Senate adjourned for the day, Mason muttered, "The senator is *non compos mentis* [not of sound mind]."

Douglas was especially incensed by the speech, not only because he had been maligned but also because the insults were deliberate. Sumner had written the speech, practiced it, and had it printed. They were not some chance remarks that had flown out in the heat of an argument.

Butler was not present to hear himself so excoriated. His cousin, Congressman Preston Brooks, was present for the first half of the speech but not for the worst remarks on the second day. Someone told Brooks the gist of the speech, and the South Carolina congressman got a copy and read it for himself, twice, to be sure there was no mistaking its intent.

Brooks was no firebrand. He was recognized as a moderate in the House of Representatives, but he could not let this insult to his kinsman and to his entire state go unchallenged. When his uncle returned to Washington, he would be forced as a man of honor to flog Sumner, but Butler was old and frail. It was up to Brooks to avenge his family's honor.

A lawsuit for slander would take too long. He considered challenging Sumner to a duel, but that would have meant recognizing the Massachusetts senator as an equal. In addition, it might be reported to the police, since dueling was against the law. He thought of bringing a rawhide whip to lash Sumner, but Sumner was six feet, four inches tall and heavily built—four inches taller and many pounds heavier than Brooks. What if Sumner seized the whip and turned it on him?

He decided on a caning, just a few blows to satisfy his uncle's honor. He chose a cane made of gutta-percha, a gum-like substance that hardens into a lightweight shape. The cane he chose tapered from one inch in diameter at the top to three-quarters of an inch at its tip, and was hollow. It weighed just over eleven ounces, including its gold head.

Thus equipped, on May 21 he waited outside the Senate chamber for Sumner, but the senator didn't appear. The following day, he went at noon to the Senate, which was being adjourned due to the death of a congressman. Accompanying him were Congressmen

Henry Edmundson of Virginia and Lawrence Keitt of South Carolina, who both knew of his plan. Keitt went behind a screen while
the Senate chamber emptied. Edmundson talked with a friend
outside while Brooks went in.

Sumner was sitting at his desk alone, busily franking copies
of his "Crime against Kansas" speech (signing the copies so that
they could be mailed free of postage). Brooks approached and said,
"I have read your speech twice over carefully. It is a libel on South
Carolina and on Mr. Butler, who is a relative of mine." He struck
Sumner lightly with the cane, and as Sumner threw up his arms
to defend himself, Brooks lost his temper and struck again and
again, shattering the cane. He pulled Sumner up by his lapel with
one hand and struck with the other.

Sumner's desk was bolted to the floor, but with the pressure
of his thighs he tore it free and rolled away from Brooks, bleeding from several cuts. He staggered into the aisle and fell, while
observers rushed to catch him and ease his fall and others grappled with Brooks. Stephen Douglas came out from a chamber, but
seeing what was happening, stepped back. He later said, "My relations with Mr. Sumner were such that if I came into the hall, my
motives would have been misconstrued." And perhaps he was glad
to see his insulter beaten.

The whole attack had taken only a minute. Brooks was surrounded, proclaiming, "I didn't mean to kill him. I only meant to
whip him." He and Keitt left the chamber. He was arrested for
assault but was freed on $500 bond.

Sumner had again changed parties, becoming a member of
the newly formed Republican Party, and in the days following, the
Republican caucus decided not to make the attack a party matter. Henry Wilson, recently elected senator from Massachusetts,
condemned the attack and demanded vindication of the honor
and dignity of the Senate. Senator Seward called for the appointment of a committee to investigate. On May 28 the committee
announced that it had no jurisdiction, since Brooks was a member
of the House.

Meanwhile, Sumner had been led out of the Senate and taken in a carriage to his lodgings, where Dr. Cornelius Boyle cleaned his wounds and put two stitches in each.

The attack produced an uproar in both the North and the South. In Massachusetts, Sumner was declared a martyr, and while he might have lost the upcoming election, he was now assured of maintaining his seat. Editorials blamed the entire South and declared that the attack would be avenged. Sumner, they asserted, was just exercising his guaranteed right of freedom of speech. There were, however, a few who said it "served him right" and "it was not half what he deserved."

In the South, naturally, the reaction was the opposite. Brooks was a hero for beating such a vitriolic man. New canes were sent to him, one with the message inscribed, "Hit him again."

As in the North, opinion was not unanimous. The Memphis *Bulletin,* while admitting that Sumner was a "low, wicked demagogue," still said that the attack could not be excused. Some Southern editors thought that Brooks had acted cowardly by attacking a sitting man, and others recognized that the attack would only inflame the Republicans in the North.

Brooks challenged Senator Wilson to a duel, but it was declined. The House investigating committee recommended that Brooks be expelled, but the measure lacked the necessary two-thirds vote. Edmundson, who had stayed out in the lobby during the attack, was acquitted. Keitt, who had threatened another senator who attempted to break up the fight, was censured. Brooks and Keitt resigned from the House and returned to South Carolina, where both were quickly reelected.

Congressman Anson Burlingame, a friend of Sumner's from Boston, who feared that he might lose the upcoming election, made the most inflammatory speeches in the House, accusing Brooks of sneaking up on Sumner and striking him from behind. When Brooks challenged him to a duel, Burlingame accepted, on the condition that he could choose the location: the Canadian side of Niagara Falls. Brooks had to decline, as he feared he would be killed on the way across Northern territory.

Brooks died within a year of a liver ailment, and soon after Senator Butler also died.

Sumner lived on. His wounds became infected and had to be drained, but he recovered. He went to mountain resorts and even to Europe to rest up and recuperate. He was reelected to the Senate, although it was three years before he attended full time. He did show up occasionally, usually summoned for a special vote, but each such occasion was followed by "nervous collapse." (We might say now that he was suffering from post-traumatic stress disorder.)

He was back in the Senate full time when Lincoln was elected and pushed for the emancipation of slaves. Because of his travels abroad and his facility with languages, he hoped to become secretary of state, but that position went to the more moderate William Seward. Sumner instead was head of the Foreign Relations Committee, which he said would control events more than the secretary of state could.

After the surrender at Appomattox in April 1865 and Lincoln's assassination, Sumner became the leader of the Radical Republicans, intent on punishing the South for the war. By secession the states had ceased to become states and were to be treated as conquered territories, he thought. He led the impeachment of President Andrew Johnson, and the beleaguered president narrowly missed being removed from office.

Sumner was still in the Senate, still in charge of the Foreign Relations Committee during the presidency of Ulysses Grant, who disliked him intensely. He sabotaged Grant's attempt to annex Santo Domingo and almost caused a war with Britain over payment of damages claimed because of Britain's support of the Confederacy. He presented Britain with a huge bill and demanded Canada as payment. The Canadians didn't want to be annexed. The matter was settled by arbitration at a conference in Geneva, Switzerland. President Grant managed to have Sumner deposed as chairman of the Foreign Relations Committee.

Sumner finally married in his fifties, to a vivacious widow, Alice Mason Hooper, half his age. They were incompatible: He lacked a sense of humor, and she had a terrible temper. She claimed he was impotent ("as limp as a dishrag") and began attending social functions with someone else. In 1873, after seven years of marriage, they divorced.

Sumner died the following year, on March 11, 1874, at the age of sixty-three, still a senator. A British newspaper, the *Anglo American Times*, had published a rumor in 1872 that he was planning to run for governor of Massachusetts—as a Democrat.

He had belonged to every American political party existing during his adult life, but it's doubtful the Democrats would have taken him back, after he had slandered so many of them.

SOURCES

The best source for Sumner's early life and the caning is the Pulitzer Prize–winning biography by David Donald, *Charles Sumner and the Coming of the Civil War* (New York: Alfred A. Knopf, 1960). I also read *Ordeal of the Union: A House Divided, 1852–1857* by Allen Nevins (New York: Charles Scribner's Sons, 1947); *It Happened in Washington, D.C.* by Gina de Angelis (Guilford, Conn.: Globe Pequot Press, 2004), "The Caning of Charles Sumner"; Kim Long's *The Almanac of Political Corruption, Scandals & Dirty Politics* (New York: Random House, 2007); *Fall from Grace: Sex, Scandals and Corruption in American Politics from 1702 to the Present* by Shelley Ross (New York: Random House, 1988); Geoffrey Perret's *Ulysses S. Grant—Soldier & President* (New York: The Modern Library, 1997); Michael Farquhar's *A Treasury of Great American Scandals* (New York: Penguin Books, 2003); *The Indiana Progress*, March 18, 1874, "The Nation Mourns," p. 4 (obituary notice); *Anglo American Times*, September 14, 1872, "Running for Governor of Massachusetts?", p. 10; and "Capitol Punishment— When Mudslinging in Congress Led to Actual Bloodshed," www .kevinbaker.info/c_cp, accessed December 19, 2009.

CHAPTER EIGHT

Roger Taney:
The Man with the Moonlight Mind

Roger B. Taney, chief justice of the U. S. Supreme Court, was so highly regarded for most of his career that he held two Cabinet posts and was consulted by presidents and congressmen. A U.S. attorney general described him as having "a moonlight mind." Taney, William Wirt said, "gave all the light to an issue without the glare." Others also praised the justice for his honesty and fairness.

Yet with one case near the end of his tenure on the high court, Taney reasoned and wrote as a jerk. That case was *Dred Scott v. Sandford*. In trying to placate Southern slaveholders and thus keep the South in the Union, Taney succeeded only in bringing down curses on himself and Northern anger at the South. Most of his other cases are long forgotten, but *Dred Scott v. Sandford* hangs around Taney's neck like an albatross.

Had this case come before the Supreme Court a decade or more earlier, Taney would probably have ruled differently. Although he was born into a slave-holding family, he had educated and freed his own slaves, and provided for the care of two older, frail slaves in their last years. What brought him to the point of making such an inflammatory ruling as he did in 1857?

Taney's ancestors had come to America as indentured servants but had managed by hard work and luck to acquire land in Calvert County, Maryland, and become prosperous. Succeeding generations bought enough land that the sons could each have a farm, but by the time Roger was born in 1777, land was more expensive, and Roger was a frail boy who was uninterested in becoming a farmer.

After attending local primary schools, Roger had a series of tutors. The family was Catholic, as were many Marylanders, but

Justice Roger Taney, who ruined a distinguished reputation with one dreadful decision.
LIBRARY OF CONGRESS

there was no Catholic school available, so Roger was sent to Dickinson College in Carlisle, Pennsylvania. It took a week to make the journey by boat and wagon, and in addition to his books and clothing, Roger had to take along enough hard money—the states did not accept each other's paper money, which fluctuated in value—to pay his expenses. He only returned home for a visit once in three years.

Roger was voted valedictorian of his class, and while he appreciated the honor, he hated making the obligatory speech, a dread that would follow him throughout his life. Following graduation he went to Annapolis to read law and during his first case was shaking so badly he could barely stand.

He returned to Calvert County where he was elected to the state legislature in his father's place. Roger thought of himself as a Federalist and opposed the changes the Democratic Republicans brought about in Maryland: the secret ballot, dividing the state into districts, expanding the right to vote, and having all districts vote on the same day. In the election of 1800, Federalists were swept from office, including Taney.

He moved westward to Frederick, Maryland, to practice law. The stage road from Baltimore to Cumberland passed through Frederick, so the town prospered, and so did Taney. Besides his law practice, he worked on the local newspaper, the *Fredericktown Herald*, whose editor was a Dickinson classmate. In 1803 Taney was nominated to the House of Delegates, but again Federalists lost.

In 1806 Roger married Anne Key, sister of his classmate Frank Key, better known later as Francis Scott Key. Roger and Anne's son died as an infant. Thereafter they had six daughters.

Taney's split from the Federalists came with the War of 1812. The Federalists from New England, led by Timothy Pickering, urged that region to secede from the Union, but Taney was opposed, though he disagreed with how President James Madison handled the war. The embargo on shipping, which hurt New England, also hurt Maryland, and Maryland was even invaded by the British.

Feelings ran high in Maryland. The office of the Federalist newspaper published in Baltimore, the *Federal Republican*, was broken into and destroyed. The editor and some friends holed up in a house to produce the paper, against Taney's advice. He wrote in a letter to his brother that they might be attracting a mob; and if they protected themselves with arms and any attackers were killed, they might be liable for murder. It happened as he predicted, and his letter was made public and used against the Federalists. They gave him little support in his next election, and he lost again. Thereafter, he tended more toward the Democratic Republicans.

Besides freeing his own slaves, Taney was a member of the American Colonization Society, which resettled freed slaves in West Africa, and he joined a local organization to protect the rights of free African Americans. He also defended a minister who spoke out forcefully against the evil of slavery.

In 1823 the Taney family moved to Baltimore. His reputation as an honest lawyer had spread, and he was able to earn a good living. In court he spoke simply, without gestures and without resorting to famous quotations as many lawyers did. His logic and clarity won cases for him, not his appearance or behavior. His voice was described as hollow, and he had an unkempt appearance, his clothes hanging somewhat baggily on his frail frame.

Taney, like many others, thought the presidency had been stolen from Andrew Jackson in the election of 1824, and he worked for Jackson's election in 1828. When Jackson decided to shuffle his Cabinet in 1831, he took Martin Van Buren's recommendation that Taney would make a good attorney general. Taney accepted. For a while he was also secretary of war until the appointee arrived.

As attorney general, Taney was asked for an opinion in 1831 on a case that could have had international repercussions. South Carolina law required that free black crewmen on ships must be kept in jail while their ships were in harbor and only released when the ships departed. Britain protested that these men were British citizens and that they had the right to go freely among the inhabitants of port cities. To forbid them to do so violated a treaty between Britain and the United States. Taney argued that the trade treaty did not mention the treatment of people, and while

South Carolina had a right to protect her slaves, other states had made laws that freed any slaves brought within their boundaries. States could make laws that pertained to themselves and their property, and the federal government had no right to interfere. He deplored slavery, he said, and he had recently bought, educated, and freed a slave, but he upheld states' rights.

Taney's attention turned away from slavery to the Second Bank of the United States. Bank manager Nicholas Biddle wanted it rechartered. Jackson thought a single bank and its branches had too much power and asked Taney's advice on what to do about the bank.

Taney advised Jackson to veto the bill on the grounds that the Second Bank of the United States was unconstitutional. He thought it was not "necessary" (it had been chartered on the grounds that the government had the right to do what is "necessary and proper" to carry out its duties). Furthermore, he stated, it gave the government a monopoly; the government had no right to establish banks in states without their permission; the bank could be used for political purposes; it was enriching private interests unfairly; and the Second Bank of the United States could ruin a city by destroying its local bank. Jackson vetoed the bank bill.

Biddle called in loans from state banks, forcing them to also call in loans, and he refused to release funds to pay the government's debt.

Jackson demanded that Secretary of the Treasury William Duane turn over all government funds. Duane refused. Jackson fired him and made Taney the acting secretary of the treasury. Taney turned over the funds, which were placed in various state banks. Many made loans with the government money and became overextended.

Taney was vilified. Congressman George McDuffie said of Taney, "He is one of those miserable sycophants who crawled in their own slime to the footstool of Executive favor."

When the Supreme Court was asked for an opinion on removing funds, Justice Joseph Story said that the funds could be removed for any reason, so long as it was reported to Congress.

Biddle said, "Nothing but public suffering will affect Congress," and set out to squeeze the economy and destroy state banks. Jackson was criticized for the resulting recession, as well as Biddle.

In the Senate, Daniel Webster, John C. Calhoun, and Henry Clay spread rumors that Taney was corrupt and that the economy was in a downslide, due to his and Jackson's mismanagement. They demanded a report on the economy. Taney went over the figures and found that the financial situation of the country was up in 1834, not down. He called Senator Thomas Hart Benton to his home, gave him the news, and turned over the report to Webster. Webster began reading the report aloud to the Senate, then realized it was favorable and stopped. Benton demanded that he read it in its entirety. The angry triumvirate rejected the appointment of Taney as secretary of the treasury, not just acting secretary, without giving a reason.

Some senators confided to Taney that they had opposed him because of Biddle's pressure but would support him for some other position. Taney replied that he could not trust his honor to the keeping of those who had already forfeited their own. For the next two years he returned to private law practice.

When Chief Justice John Marshall died in 1835, President Jackson nominated Taney to fill that position. A second justice died and Philip Barbour of Virginia was nominated to fill the vacancy. Since no two justices could serve from the same judicial circuit, the Senate tried to block Taney's appointment by combining the two districts and then dividing them to create a new one that contained both Maryland and Virginia. The scheme was foiled by James Buchanan, who brought the appointments forward before the redistricting could be presented, and both nominees were confirmed.

Taney wrote after the confirmation, "My political battles are over, and I must devote myself to the calm but high duties of the station to which I am honored." But he was wrong. Case after case would be presented that would result in further "battles."

The Taney court gave corporations the right to move cases from state to federal courts if more than one state was involved.

He held too that states must abide by the contracts they had made, even if they were made foolishly.

The slavery issue arose again in the case of *Groves v. Slaughter.* Slaughter, a Mississippi resident, had bought slaves from a Louisiana seller but refused to pay for them, claiming that his purchase was void, since Mississippi had outlawed the importation of slaves. Justice John McLean held that since slaves were both people and objects of purchase they were excluded from the power of the federal government to regulate as interstate commerce. Taney went further: Each state might decide for itself, without interference from the federal government, whether it would admit slaves from other states. Further, states could vote to abolish slavery, or if they had it, vote to keep it. But Slaughter must return the slaves to their seller.

The *Amistad* case also involved slavery. A shipload of slaves was sold in Havana, Cuba, against Spanish law, then sent to another port. On that second voyage the slaves seized control of the ship *Amistad* and sailed it to Connecticut. Since this was a free state, they declared their freedom. Taney's court ruled in favor of the slaves, not because setting foot in a free state ended bondage, but because Spanish law had been broken and because the slaves were kidnapped from Africa to start with.

In the *Prigg* case, a Maryland man had gone to Pennsylvania, seized a former slave, and taken her back to Maryland without waiting for legal permission from Pennsylvania. Pennsylvania had a law requiring an investigation because slave traders sometimes seized free blacks, claiming they were slaves. Taney's court upheld the Fugitive Slave Law of 1793. States might make laws pertaining to slavery, as long as they did not conflict with federal law.

Questions on slavery continued to be brought before Taney, in increasing numbers as succeeding administrations tackled the issue. Following Jackson's administration, Martin Van Buren served one term as president. The aged general William Henry Harrison, a Whig, was elected in 1840, but died of pneumonia only a month after his inaugural. His successor was the unknown John

Tyler of Virginia, who disliked Taney for his support of Jackson. Taney was delighted when James K. Polk, called "Young Hickory" because of his expansionist policies, was elected president in 1844. The United States added territory as a result of war with Mexico, and the southwestern land meant a possibility of more slave states. The Compromise of 1850 was an attempt to settle which territories would have slaves and which would not, but the issue would not stay settled.

In 1854 the Kansas-Nebraska Act was passed, setting the terms under which those two territories might choose to enter the Union as slave or free states. Partisans of each side rushed to the territories, and local warfare broke out. The slavery issue remained incendiary.

Taney attempted to put the issue aside, spend time with his family, contemplate what he had accomplished, and write his autobiography. After all, he was old. How much longer would he serve on the Supreme Court? He, his wife, Anne, and two unmarried daughters were vacationing at Old Point Comfort, at Hampton, Virginia, in the summer of 1855, when Taney began writing. An outbreak of yellow fever hit the port of Norfolk, spread to Portsmouth and then across the river to Hampton, with devastating results. Hundreds died, including Anne Taney and their daughter Alice. A grief-stricken Taney laid aside his autobiography, never to pick it up again, and returned to Washington. He had lost his beloved companion but still had the responsibility of an unmarried daughter, a divorced daughter, and an unsuccessful son-in-law who often borrowed money. Taney was approaching eighty years of age, in a prestigious but mediocre-paying position, with little opportunity to earn more.

If he had known what lay ahead, he should have resigned from the Supreme Court and spent his last years shoring up his finances, for his legal reputation was about to be ruined by a single case.

The case of *Dred Scott v. Sandford* had been making its way through the courts for years and was sent to the Supreme Court in 1856.

Dred Scott was a slave owned by a Virginian, Peter Blow, who moved with his family and slaves to Missouri. Following Blow's death two years later, Scott was sold to Dr. John Emerson, an army surgeon. For three years Emerson was posted to Rock Island, Illinois. Scott was taken along and worked for the doctor. Emerson then took Scott to his new post in Minnesota. Here Scott was married to Harriet Robinson, a former slave. The Scotts had two children.

Soon after his return with the Scotts to Missouri, Emerson died, and the Scott family became part of the doctor's estate, which passed to his widow. Dred Scott attempted to buy his freedom from the widow, but his offer was refused. He sued in the Missouri courts for his freedom, claiming that since he had been taken into Illinois, a state that prohibited slavery, he was automatically freed. In addition, Minnesota had been designated a free territory by the terms of the Missouri Compromise. Residence in either would make him free. The trial court ruled in Scott's favor, but Irene Emerson appealed to the Missouri Supreme Court and by the time the case was heard in 1852, attitudes had hardened. Earlier, states had accepted the principle of *comity*, that is, status in one state meant the same status in another. (For example, a couple married in one state according to its laws would be considered married in all other states as well.).

The Missouri Supreme Court ruled that a free state had no right to change the status of a slave. With the encouragement of his previous owners, the Blow family, Scott appealed to the U.S. Supreme Court. Mrs. Emerson had turned her financial and legal affairs over to her brother, John Sandford, so the case became *Dred Scott v. Sandford.*

The Taney court could have let the ruling of the lower court stand, or overturned it with limited comments, or refused to hear it altogether. It did neither. The court had five Southern justices and four from the North. Taney thought that by issuing a ruling favorable to the South, he could prevent that region from seceding from the Union. The case arrived in 1856 and was postponed first because of the death of Justice Peter V. Daniel's wife in a fire and then by a rehearing.

James Buchanan, elected president in November 1856, asked in late February 1857 what the Court's decision was, and on learning it, asked that announcement of it be postponed until after his inauguration. When the chief justice chatted with the president-elect before the gathered crowd just before administering the oath of office, critics assumed that Taney was telling him the Court's decision. Buchanan already knew it but spoke as if he did not: "I shall cheerfully submit to the decision of the Court, whatever it might be."

Taney's opinion gave the Scott case the full treatment, going back to the condition of slaves at the time the Constitution was written. The Founding Fathers had accepted slavery, providing for the end of the importation of slaves but not the end of slavery itself. They had recognized them as inferior, Taney wrote, not as people likely to become citizens. Dred Scott was thus not a citizen and could not sue in the courts. Taney ignored the fact that Scott had married in a civil, legal ceremony, an indication that he was considered a citizen, since marriages between slaves were not recognized as legal. Taney also ignored the fact that throughout American history free blacks had been considered citizens, with the right to vote. Some indeed may have voted for those who ratified the Constitution.

As if these statements were not inflammatory enough, Taney further held that the Missouri Compromise was unconstitutional and that only the states and not the federal government could make laws forbidding slavery. Moreover, if Scott had been freed by residence in a free state, that state would be guilty of taking property without "due process" of law. Since Scott was property and not a citizen, he must remain a slave.

Ironically, Scott was freed by his owner soon after the case concluded.

The North was outraged at Taney's decision, and the case became a major issue in the election of 1860. The South seceded anyway, and the terrible Civil War was fought.

During the war Taney ruled in his capacity as a circuit judge that President Lincoln was wrong to suspend *habeas corpus*—the right to be charged and given the opportunity for bail—even in time of war. He accomplished nothing by this except angering Lincoln.

Taney lived on until the Civil War was almost over, dying on October 12, 1864. The year before, Senator Benjamin Wade confided to another senator that he had prayed for Taney to live past Buchanan's term in office, so Buchanan would not be able to appoint his successor, but since Taney lived on, "I fear I have overdone my prayers."

Many abolitionists celebrated Taney's death, and Charles Sumner of Massachusetts said, "The name of Taney is to be hooted down the pages of history." Of the president's Cabinet, only Secretary of State William Seward, Postmaster General William Dennison, and Attorney General Edward Bates attended the funeral service at Taney's home, along with the president and the Taney family. Bates accompanied the family to Frederick for the burial.

A proposal to place a bust of Taney in the Supreme Court was passed by the House of Representatives but rejected in the Senate, largely due to Senator Sumner. Ten years later, in 1874, after the death of Taney's successor, Chief Justice Salmon Chase, busts of both men were placed in the Supreme Court building.

Sources

I read Carl Brent Swisher's classic, *Roger B. Taney* (New York: Macmillan, 1935) as well as James F. Simon's *Lincoln and Chief Justice Taney: Slavery, Secession and the President's War Powers* (New York: Simon & Schuster, 2006) and Judge Andrew Napolitano's *Dred Scott's Revenge* (Nashville, Tenn.: Thomas Nelson Co., 2009). The Dred Scott case is retold in *The Emergence of Lincoln, Douglas, Buchanan and Party Chaos, 1857–1859* by Allan Nevins (New York: Charles Scribner's Sons, 1950). Taney also shows up in biographies of Andrew Jackson, James Buchanan, John C. Calhoun, Daniel Webster, Henry Clay, and other of his contemporaries.

One shot turned John Wilkes Booth from popular actor to hunted killer.
LIBRARY OF CONGRESS

CHAPTER NINE

John Wilkes Booth:
The Jerk Who Changed History

The destinies of two of the best-known men in America came together on the night of April 14, 1865, making one a beloved martyr, the other an infamous outlaw, and resulting in the death of both. One was Abraham Lincoln, president of the United States, out for an evening's entertainment with his wife to celebrate General Robert E. Lee's surrender five days before, effectively ending the Civil War. The other was popular Shakespearean actor John Wilkes Booth, younger son of a famous acting family.

Lincoln had received the most votes in the election of 1860, but very few in the South voted for him. From the time news of his election spread, he began to get death threats, and there were some ineffectual attempts on his life.

Before he could take office in March 1861, seven Southern states seceded from the Union and were later joined by four others to form the Confederate States of America. Maryland, which surrounded the District of Columbia on three sides, did not secede, but the southern part of the state was strongly sympathetic to the Confederacy. When it was known that Lincoln would be changing trains in Baltimore on his way from Illinois to Washington, a group of Confederates plotted to kidnap him between stations. They were ready when the eastbound train pulled into Baltimore, but the president was not on board. The plot had been discovered, and Lincoln had made the trip nine hours earlier.

Lincoln had a fatalistic outlook on life. What God willed would happen. He told friends that he realized anyone who wanted to kill him could do so, provided the killer was willing to sacrifice his own life. No president of the United States had been murdered. Lincoln would become the first.

In April 1861 war began between the Union and the Confederacy. Their capitals, Washington and Richmond, were only a hundred miles apart. Lincoln at first thought he could end the war within weeks by sending an army to capture Richmond. The Washington elite went out with picnic lunches to watch the Confederacy be defeated, but the Battle of First Manassas ended in a Union retreat. The war wore on with neither side able to achieve a decisive victory.

Then Lincoln issued the Emancipation Proclamation, stating that slaves in states still in rebellion were freed and could join the Union army. This led to panic in the South. Owners feared their families would be massacred. Moreover, slaves and the land they tilled represented the South's major wealth. Confederate President Jefferson Davis issued a statement that any freed blacks who had joined the Union army and were captured would be executed. Lincoln issued a counter statement that for each black executed, a Confederate prisoner would be executed. Neither man actually followed through on his threats, but large numbers of troops on both sides were taken prisoner, and each side began to scheme how they might free their imprisoned troops.

Twice in 1864 Lincoln sent forces to take Richmond, free the prisoners, and "capture President Davis." The first attack turned back, not realizing how poorly Richmond was defended. The second attempt was discovered by the Confederate troops and turned back at the Chicahominy River. The object was clear: to free the 13,000 Union soldiers at Libby Prison in Richmond (where one of the wardens was Mary Todd Lincoln's brother David) and capture President Davis. Then Dahlgren's Raid also failed, but this time there was written proof of the Union's intent. One group of forces was armed with oakum, turpentine, and torpedoes, with instructions to burn the city. Documents found in Colonel Ulric Dahlgren's handwriting stated that prisoners were to be freed, Richmond burned, and "Davis and his cabinet killed."

This was a different kind of warfare. Confederates in turn planned to capture Lincoln and hold him for ransom until all Confederate prisoners were freed.

Where did John Wilkes Booth fit into the plans?

John was the younger son of a famous theatrical family. His father, Junius Booth, was a popular actor in England when he decided to abandon his wife and son and immigrate to America with Mary Ann Holmes, pregnant with their first son, Junius Jr. The Booths settled in Baltimore and Junius Sr. was soon performing on American stages. He was well paid and bought a home in Bel Air, Maryland, for his growing family. Junius Booth Jr., called June, became an actor, as did the next son, Edwin. Edwin traveled with his father, attempting to keep him sober. The acting trio earned substantial fees performing for miners in California after the 1849 Gold Rush, and Junius Sr. set out on the return to Maryland alone. He was robbed, then got a fever—probably typhoid—and died before reaching home. Edwin and June went on acting and soon young John began to appear on stage as well.

John quickly became popular, especially with women, though men too reported that he could charm people into doing his bidding. He earned high fees for acting and spent money freely, especially on lavish costumes for plays. At the time of the assassination, he was carrying in his wallet pictures of five young women and was engaged to Lucy Hale, the daughter of a former senator who had just been named ambassador to Spain.

One of John's favorite cities was Richmond, Virginia. He felt at ease in the Southern city and appreciated the Southern way of life. In 1859, while he was performing in Richmond, he saw militia gathering at the railroad station, ready to go to Harper's Ferry in northwestern Virginia, where the abolitionist John Brown was to be hanged for leading a slave uprising. Booth wanted to see the execution, to make sure Brown's followers didn't rescue him, and he managed to talk his way into becoming a temporary militiaman. He acted the part well and witnessed the hanging, though he admitted he admired the stoicism of Brown and felt faint at the sight of the dead body twisting on the scaffold.

When war began, the Booth family split, like many other American families. Edwin was firmly pro-Union and forbade

John, the Southern sympathizer, to stay at his house when he was present. John could visit their mother if Edwin was away. Somewhere John encountered Confederate activists and joined forces with them. June remained in California, and Joseph, the youngest Booth brother, went to Australia.

While the Union forces were attempting to take Richmond and kidnap or kill President Jefferson Davis, the Confederates hatched schemes of their own. One involved infecting people in Northern cities with yellow fever germs, carried—they thought—by the clothing of victims who had died of the fever. Several trunks of such clothes were shipped from Bermuda following an outbreak, but no epidemics occurred from the clothing.

Another scheme, which John Wilkes Booth helped plan, was to kidnap Lincoln when he rode alone from the White House to the "cottage" on the grounds of the Soldiers' Home, where the Lincolns often went to be undisturbed. The president would be taken through southern Maryland to Virginia and held until imprisoned Confederate troops were released. Lee's Army of Northern Virginia was dwindling, and freed prisoners could bolster the army.

By this time in 1864, Booth had gathered a group of conspirators. Some he had met in Canada, some in New York, and others he'd been introduced to in Maryland. Booth wanted to move ahead with the kidnapping quickly. His aim was not just to release prisoners by kidnapping the president but also to do the deed himself and get credit for it. At a meeting in Baltimore in August 1864, he enlisted longtime school friends Samuel Arnold and Michael O'Laughlen, both former Confederate soldiers, in the plot.

This scheme fell through when troops began accompanying the president. Next the group planned to commandeer Lincoln's carriage when he was en route to make a speech, but the president's schedule changed at the last minute.

In Montreal Booth met Patrick Martin, an important Confederate agent, who gave him letters of introduction to Confederate contacts in Charles County, Maryland, including Dr. Samuel Mudd. Mary Surratt's former tavern, at Surrattsville, only thirteen miles from Washington, was a well-known safe house on the courier route from Richmond to Montreal, and Booth arranged to stay there. Twice in late 1864 Booth met with Dr. Mudd. He also stayed at the Surratt boardinghouse in Washington, D.C.

Events moved more swiftly than the conspirators planned. The Confederacy was crumbling, and her armies were on the run. Something had to be done quickly. At this point Booth's plans probably changed from kidnapping to murder. He cashed out some investments, made bequests to his brother June and sister Rosalie, and wrote letters justifying what he was about to do, entrusting them to his sister Asia to lock up for safekeeping and later release.

The final blow to the Southern cause as far as Booth was concerned came when General Robert E. Lee surrendered his army to General Ulysses Grant at Appomattox, Virginia. President Davis had fled first to Danville, Virginia, and then to Greensboro, North Carolina, but would also soon surrender. Celebrations were going on all over the Union, but especially in Washington. Booth now expanded his plan to include assassinating not only President Lincoln but also Vice President Andrew Johnson and Secretary of State William Seward, who was then next in the line of succession. With the U.S. government effectively destroyed, the South might have another chance.

The assassination should be done at a theater, he decided, where he could move freely, accepted and thus not suspected. He was doubly pleased to learn that General Grant and his wife would be joining the Lincolns at a play at Ford's Theatre on April 14. The date was the anniversary of the fall of Fort Sumter, and at a ceremony that day the flag of the United States was once more hoisted above the fort. It was thus a significant day for several reasons. Booth was pleased. He could not only kill the president but the leading Union general as well.

During the day Booth sent his field glass and a message to John Lloyd, who ran Surratt's Tavern, to "have the guns ready" and delivered by Mary Surratt. The two guns and some ammunition had been hidden at the tavern ready for the aborted March 17 kidnap attempt. Booth picked up his mail at Ford's Theatre and scoped out the premises, planning just how he would carry out the murder. He arranged to rent a horse, and confirmed the conspirators' assignments. George Atzerodt, who had checked into the Kirkwood Hotel where Vice President Johnson was staying, was assigned to kill Johnson. Lewis Powell, a former soldier who had been captured, sworn allegiance to the Union, and released, was to kill Secretary of State Seward. Davey Herold was to accompany Powell.

Booth had been introduced to John Surratt, Mary's son, by Dr. Mudd outside Mary's boardinghouse in Washington. Another boarder there was Louis Weichmann, who was to provide valuable evidence for the prosecution at the conspirators' trials.

After the attacks the conspirators were to meet at Soper's Hill in Maryland, near the home of Dr. Mudd.

The plans soon went awry. Atzerodt spent the afternoon in a bar drinking himself into a stupor and failed to make even a token effort to kill Vice President Johnson. Herold and Powell went to Seward's house but failed to kill him. Powell pretended to be delivering medicine to Seward, who had been injured in a carriage accident a few days before. Both of Seward's sons and his daughter, as well as several servants, were present and were suspicious of the "deliveryman." Powell attacked wildly, knocking Frederick Seward unconscious and slashing the face of the secretary of state so badly that he nearly bled to death.

Not waiting for Powell, Herold rode off for his rendezvous with Booth.

Booth left his horse in the rear alley behind the theater, made his way underneath the stage while the play was in progress, and came out the front. Doorkeepers nodded to him, used to seeing him at the theater. He had a drink at a bar next door, then casually reentered the theater. He presented his card to one of the guards, who let him enter the dress circle where the presidential box was.

The comedy, *Our American Cousin,* was already in progress when the Lincolns arrived. The Grants had declined, saying that they wanted to catch an early train to New Jersey to visit their children. It was no secret in Washington that Mrs. Grant—along with many others—disliked Mary Lincoln, and this may have been a second or even main reason for declining the invitation. Secretary of War Edwin Stanton and his wife were then invited, but they declined. Finally Major Henry Rathbone and his fiancée, Clara Harris, accompanied the Lincolns.

Booth entered the vestibule leading to the presidential box and stood in the shadows, waiting for the right moment. He quietly stepped into the presidential box, braced the door closed, and took out his derringer. At a point in the play when the audience laughed loudly, Booth fired, not more than two feet behind the president. The bullet entered the back of Lincoln's skull, and he slumped forward, mortally wounded.

Booth slashed out at Major Rathbone, who attempted to stop his escape, and leaped over the balustrade of the box. As he did so, his spur caught in the flags draped over the box, throwing him off balance. He landed on the stage awkwardly, all his weight on one leg, which snapped. He stood, raised his arms, and cried, "Sic semper tyrannis!" (Thus always to tyrants.)

Outside, he grabbed his horse and rode for the Navy Yard Bridge. When sentries stopped him, he gave his real name and told them he was heading for Beantown, Maryland. This was near Dr. Mudd's home. Booth was making no attempt to hide what he had done or who he was. The sentries let him pass with the warning that he could not reenter the city until daylight. He said he didn't intend to. A few minutes later Herold approached the same bridge, gave a fake name and destination, and said that he had stayed overlong "with a lady of the night." He too was let past with the same warning. Soon after midnight Booth and Herold met at Soper's Hill, went to Surratt's Tavern for the field glass and guns, and rode off toward Dr. Mudd's house.

Meanwhile, the unconscious Lincoln was taken to a nearby house owned by William Petersen, where several doctors gathered to examine him. They cut off his clothing and determined that the bullet wound to the head was his only injury, but it had pierced the brain and broken the right eye socket. His face began to swell, and his breathing was shallow and uneven. Nothing could be done for him.

Secretary of War Stanton heard of the attack on Seward and raced to his house, only to learn on the way of Lincoln's murder. He went to the Petersen house and took charge of the government, sending telegrams and organizing the early investigation and search for the assassins. Several witnesses had recognized Booth, and by 3 a.m. Stanton sent out a telegram naming him as the killer. He didn't know then, but suspected, that the attack on Seward was related.

One of the first steps was to ascertain the safety of Vice President Johnson and prepare him for his approaching responsibility. Officers who went to the Kirkwood Hotel asked if any unusual people had been around. The clerk took them to Atzerodt's room, where they found in his coat a bankbook belonging to John Wilkes Booth.

At a few minutes after 7 a.m. on April 15, Abraham Lincoln died. The largest manhunt in history to that time had already begun.

Booth and Herold went to Dr. Mudd's home, awoke him, and demanded that he tend Booth's broken leg, which had swelled and was making it difficult for him to ride. The doctor cut off the boot, tended the leg, and soon sent the pair on their way. Several days later he told a relative that "a stranger" had come after his horse had thrown him, causing him to break a bone in his leg. After hearing of the assassination, Mudd said, he realized that the "stranger" might be the man the military officers were seeking.

Over the next twelve days, Booth and Herold were aided by several sympathizers, hid out in Zekiah Swamp, were ferried across the Potomac River (mistakenly to a point of land still in Maryland), then reached King George County, Virginia, the following day. They had encountered four Confederate soldiers returning from the war, and Herold confessed who he and Booth were.

One of the soldiers, Willie Jett, directed them to the farm of Richard Garrett. He was later to lead federal troops to Garrett's barn where Booth and Herold were hiding.

When the troops torched the barn, Booth called out that Herold wanted to surrender. The barn door opened, and Herold walked out and was arrested. Although orders were to bring Booth in alive, one of the men, Boston Corbett, shot him. Booth was dragged out of the burning barn, paralyzed from the neck down by the shot that had pierced his spine. He died a few minutes later. His body was sewn into a blanket and taken upriver to Washington, where it was identified by federal authorities and buried beneath the prison yard where four of his coconspirators—Mary Surratt, Davey Herold, Lewis Powell, and George Atzerodt—were soon hanged.

Booth's coconspirators are hanged just above where his body was temporarily buried.
LIBRARY OF CONGRESS

Given the hysteria following Lincoln's assassination, the accused were tried immediately, found guilty on July 6, and hanged the following day.

What of the others who saw something or knew something of the assassination? Louis Weichmann went to the authorities and was a star witness against the conspirators he had known at the boardinghouse. Dr. Samuel Mudd, Samuel Arnold, and Michael O'Laughlen were sentenced to life imprisonment at Fort Jefferson off the Florida Keys. Edman Spangler, whose only participation in the assassination had been to open the theater door when Booth tapped on it, and who watched Booth's horse until he could turn it over to someone else, was sentenced to six years in the same prison.

Booth family members received death threats, and when Edwin Booth got permission from President Johnson to bury his brother in an unmarked grave in the family plot, the Episcopal minister who conducted the service was fired by his congregation. Edwin Booth never again went to Washington, D.C., and on the day of his funeral in 1893, the roof of Ford's Theatre collapsed, killing twenty people.

John Surratt, Mary's son, fled to Canada, to England, and then to Rome, where he became a zouave for the Vatican. He was turned in by someone from his childhood who recognized him. Surratt fled to Egypt, where he was arrested and brought back to the United States for trial. He was acquitted. He married, gave several lectures about the assassination, and eventually had a teaching career.

President Andrew Johnson pardoned the four sent to Fort Jefferson, but O'Laughlen had died.

Mary Lincoln, always high-strung and paranoid, eventually became insane, and her son Robert had to take over her finances and have her committed to an institution. Even the engaged pair in the presidential box were affected. They married and had three children, but Rathbone's behavior became erratic. Accusing his wife of infidelity, he shot her, then stabbed her, and committed suicide.

John Wilkes Booth, claiming to be acting to benefit the South, actually did the South a bad turn. Had Lincoln lived, his treatment of the conquered states would have been kinder than that meted out by the Radical Republicans.

SOURCES

So much has been written about President Abraham Lincoln and John Wilkes Booth that it was difficult to summarize this historical event in one chapter. The books I referred to are the following: The earliest published source I consulted was *The Man Who Killed Lincoln: The Story of John Wilkes Booth and His Part in the Assassination* by Philip Van Doren Stern (New York: Literary Guild of America, 1939). Stern recreates dialogue to give "local color" for the time and place, and attempts a psychological study of Booth's motives. *The Day Lincoln Was Shot* by Jim Bishop (New York: Bantam Books, 1955) gives an hour-by-hour recounting of the events of April 14, 1865. It is useful, though later research shows Bishop made a few mistakes. *Good Brother, Bad Brother* by James Cross Giblin gives background on the Booth family as well as traces the events of the assassination (New York: Clarion Books, 2005); Thomas Goodrich's *The Darkest Dawn: Lincoln, Booth, and the Great American Tragedy* (Bloomington: University of Indiana Press, 2005) has a great deal of information on the aftermath of the assassination and its effect on the participants and observers; Michael W. Kauffman in *American Brutus* (New York: Random House, 2004) includes letters, telegrams, and other documents related to the assassination. Kauffman, a Marylander, has lived in the Booth house and traveled the route Booth took after the assassination, and he presents some facts overlooked both by historians and by the prosecution and defense in the conspiracy trial. Edward Steers Jr. has become an expert on the assassination. His *Blood on the Moon* (Lexington: University of Kentucky Press, 2001) presents some facts to disprove earlier myths, and he helpfully included not just photos but maps of Booth's escape route and a diagram of Ford's Theatre that I found useful in understanding just where the major players in the tragedy were.

*Ulysses S. Grant's middle initial could have stood for "sucker,"
as he trusted all the wrong people.*

CHAPTER TEN

The Grant Scandals

Ulysses Grant was an honest man who never benefited from any of the schemes perpetrated by his colleagues, but because he was generous and trusting, his administration has gone down in history as one of the most corrupt, if not the most corrupt. One of the best known scandals, the Crédit Mobilier, was carried out during the administration of President Andrew Johnson, but because word of it came out during Grant's tenure, he got the blame for that also. He was not corrupt, just a sucker.

Grant was a failure at nearly every enterprise he undertook, except for having a happy marriage. He was broke and in debt when his appointment as a general in the Civil War rescued him from oblivion and poverty. When victory came, he was the nation's hero, and the obvious choice for president. He didn't want that office and didn't campaign for it, but he won twice and was even urged to run for an unprecedented third term.

Ulysses Grant's father, Jesse, was a tanner who vowed to be able to afford a wife by age twenty-five and to retire at sixty. He succeeded at both. He married Hannah Simpson, a Quaker. Jesse was a well-read man who named his and Hannah's first-born son Hiram Ulysses Grant for the Greek hero. Like his namesake, Ulysses Grant would be a wanderer.

Young Ulysses wasn't especially interested in the military, but West Point offered a chance at a good education. When a local appointee dropped out, Ulysses got his chance. The appointment papers had no middle name for him, and the clerk, knowing his mother's maiden name was Simpson, assumed that was his middle name. Ulysses protested, but he was ever after to have Simpson recorded as his middle name.

Gifted with a photographic memory, he achieved high academic marks with little studying, a trait that was to serve him well later. He hoped to join the cavalry after graduation, but in a fit of anger, he mistreated a horse. Consequently, he was put in the infantry and posted to Jefferson Barracks in Missouri. Here he met Julia Dent, the sister of a colleague, Frederick Dent. Grant fell in love with Julia, proposed, and was accepted, despite the disapproval of her slave-owning father.

Grant was assigned to the quartermaster corps and sent to Mexico. During the Mexican War his commanding officers were Zachary Taylor, soon to be president, and Winfield Scott, commander of the Union army at the beginning of the Civil War. One of his colleagues was another West Pointer, Robert E. Lee. Their paths would intersect in Virginia in 1865.

As quartermaster general, Grant was responsible for paying wages and expenses. While he was sick, a chest containing $300 was stolen. Later, a replacement chest containing $1,000 was also stolen. The second time he was made liable for the debt, a huge amount for a soldier to pay.

Grant wrote Julia long, detailed letters, and she answered sporadically. Still, he married her. Julia wanted to accompany him to his new post in California. He refused, knowing that she and their newborn son, Frederick, could not survive the long journey by ship to Panama, across the isthmus, and up the west coast. Much has been made of Grant's drinking, but his habit of drinking only wine on the terrible crossing of Panama saved his life. Nearly a third of those who began the trek died of cholera caused by drinking polluted water. Of the twenty children along on the expedition, seventeen died before reaching the Pacific and the remaining three died soon after reaching San Francisco.

In addition to his military service, Grant joined with a colleague in a mercantile business, but his partner left California with the profits. Next he tried growing potatoes to feed the gold miners, but so many others had the same idea that the price of potatoes dropped to pennies a bushel. Lonely without Julia and his son, Grant asked for a transfer, which was refused. He resigned. He arrived back at the Dent home broke and without a career. He tried farming on the land Julia had been given, and even built a house himself, but he failed at farming. Grant had no choice but to work in his father's leather business in Illinois to support his family. He was there when the Civil War began.

Grant went from office to office, trying to get a commission or to enlist in the army at a lesser rank. Finally Congressman Elihu Washburne got him a commission as a colonel. Grant borrowed money to have a uniform made and to buy a horse before setting off to his posting along the western edge of the Confederacy.

The first battles of the war, both in the East and the West, were disasters for the Union, but soon Grant's troops took Fort Donelson in Tennessee. As his army made its way down the Tennessee and Mississippi Rivers, he lost a few battles, but succeeded in taking Vicksburg and thus cutting the South's control of the Mississippi. He commandeered a pillared mansion for his residence, and Julia joined him. He was made a brigadier general.

As Lincoln replaced one commander after another, Grant's tenaciousness and strategy came to the president's attention. He put Grant in charge of the Army of the Potomac, which was assigned to take Virginia and stop Lee. Grant succeeded, resulting in the surrender of Lee's Army of Northern Virginia at Appomattox on April 9, 1865. The war was essentially over, though a few scattered battles were fought afterward.

The Grants were invited to attend the theater with the Lincolns on April 14 but declined. Ever afterward, Grant thought that if he had been in the box with the president, he might have heard the door opening and might have somehow deflected the assassin's bullet.

Grant was the nation's hero, commanding general of the army, and the first three-star general since George Washington. Andrew Johnson, Lincoln's successor, gave him an unprecedented fourth star, named him acting secretary of war, and appointed Grant's oldest son, Frederick, to West Point. Others gave the Grants more substantial rewards: a house in Galena, Illinois, one in Philadelphia, and one in Georgetown, plus $55,000 in bonds. With his improved salary as a four-star general, plus the interest on the bonds, the Grants were well fixed financially for the first time.

While the United States was engaged in the Civil War, a puppet emperor, Maximilian, had been set up in Mexico. The Mexicans overthrew the emperor and assassinated him, establishing a republic. President Johnson asked Grant to go as a diplomat to Mexico, but the general refused. He'd had enough of Mexico during his time there as quartermaster general.

Things were going well for the Grants, but not for the nation. President Johnson was impeached and narrowly missed being removed from office. Riots broke out in Memphis and several other cities, and the South chafed under harsh military occupation.

When the time came to choose a new president in 1868, the Republicans asked Grant to run. He wasn't sure he was a Republican. He'd voted for Democrat James Buchanan in 1856 and had supported Stephen Douglas in 1860, but he felt his policies were more attuned to the Republicans. He was chosen by acclamation at the Chicago convention. His running mate was Schuyler Colfax, speaker of the House of Representatives. The Democrats nominated Horatio Seymour, the former governor of New York.

The Democratic press depicted Grant as "a butcher of his own troops, a drunkard, a madman, a military dictator in waiting."

Even so, when the returns came in, Grant had won. White votes were fairly evenly split, but blacks voted overwhelmingly for Grant. He received 214 electoral votes to 80 for Seymour. Grant was forty-six years old, the youngest man elected up to that time.

The Grants sold their Georgetown house and the family, including Julia's father, moved into the White House. Julia set about redecorating it. When the social rounds of Washington became too tiring, they could go to a cottage they bought on the New Jersey shore.

Grant was a master of military strategy, not of government. He saw Congress as the major part of government, with the president's job being to carry out the will of Congress and to act as a ceremonial figurehead of the country. Having only recently become a Republican and having no strong loyalty to the party, he angered its members by choosing his Cabinet without consulting party leaders. One leading Republican, Charles Sumner, head of the Senate Foreign Relations Committee, expected to be named secretary of state. When Grant failed to offer the post to him, Sumner became Grant's implacable enemy and wrecked several possible foreign deals that Grant proposed. His choice for secretary of state, Hamilton Fish, was an excellent decision, but some of his other appointments were not. By appointing family and friends to high office without regard to party, Grant lost party support and also left himself liable for the crimes his appointees committed.

For secretary of the treasury, Grant nominated multimillionaire department store owner Alexander Stewart, despite a 1789 law that said no one in trade could hold that post. It would seem that someone "in trade" would be the very person to fill the job. Grant tried to get the law repealed and to have Stewart's assets put in a "blind trust." Grant was ahead of his time in seeking this solution. Sumner blocked the move. Reluctantly Grant turned to the Republican Party for a treasury secretary and ended up with a mediocre, forgettable choice.

Grant was determined to get rid of the Tenure of Office Act, which had led in part to the impeachment of Andrew Johnson. Grant wanted a free hand to hire and fire his subordinates and told the Republican-dominated Congress that he would not fire any government employees until the act was repealed. This meant no patronage jobs for congressmen to dispense. Congress did not repeal the act outright but made enough changes to satisfy Grant.

Before 1860 government conflict in America had been about slavery and states' rights. The Civil War settled that. Most former Confederate states were under military rule, but Grant knew that would soon come to an end. The most immediate problem, he thought, was reducing the national debt, which had grown twenty-fold because of the war. This meant calling in greenbacks issued during the war and putting the country back on the gold standard.

Grant held office during a time when many men saw nothing wrong with cheating their way to riches. A pair of these, James Fisk and Jay Gould, schemed to corner the gold market and run up its price. They entertained the president and—through the help of Abel Corbin, a financier who had married Grant's sister Virginia—convinced him that he would harm farmers and small business owners by releasing gold to buy up greenbacks. When Grant realized what was happening, he sold huge amounts of government gold, plunging the price and ruining Fisk and Gould. In the investigation that followed, they tried to implicate him in their scheme, claiming that the president had taken a $25,000 bribe and that his wife, Julia, had been given $100,000. Both charges were proven false.

A well-known scandal, the Crédit Mobilier matter, began in 1865, before Grant's election, but the investigation did not bring out the sordid facts until 1872. It involved a complicated financial maneuver that would have impressed modern-day cheats. The Union Pacific Railroad was in effect triple financed. The government gave railroad builders large sections of land that they could sell to pay for construction. The government also loaned the railroads money, which would be paid off at the end of thirty years, and contracted to haul troops, equipment, and supplies on the rail lines. Many cities and towns gave the railroads incentives to build tracks to their particular locations. In addition, Crédit Mobilier issued shares of stock at a price below its true value, and one insider, Oakes Ames, sold the shares at the low par value to congressmen. The first "dividend" to the purchasers paid for the stock, so it was free, and further dividends were sure to come in.

Congressman Washburne, who had been a friend and helper of Grant's, proposed that half the amount the government paid the railroads for haulage should go to paying off the loan sooner. Those in on the stock deal quickly defeated his proposal.

Then one of the investors quarreled with Ames and blew the whistle, listing government officials who had received stock. These included James A. Garfield, later to be elected president; James

G. Blaine, speaker of the House of Representatives and a later presidential candidate; and Schuyler Colfax, vice president. Grant had nothing to do with the scheme and had had no say in Colfax's nomination, but the Crédit Mobilier affair was referred to as another of "Grant's scandals." Colfax was dumped when Grant ran for reelection in 1872.

Grant had chosen as his private secretary (now called chief of staff) Orville Babcock, who had served in the army with him. At the same time, Babcock was superintendent of public buildings. He was implicated in several different scandals.

Because of his experience crossing Panama with the army, Grant wanted a sea-to-sea canal and sent seven survey crews to look for a good route. If such a canal were possible, it would be good to secure territory in the Caribbean for a naval base. The place he had in mind, Santo Domingo (now the Dominican Republic), could also serve as a refuge for freed blacks who did not want to live in the Southern states. Grant sent Babcock to Santo Domingo in an attempt to buy the territory, but because of corruption at both ends, that attempt failed. He tried again in 1871 with a treaty that gave the residents there the right to vote on their fate, but Senator Sumner opposed the treaty and kept it from passing.

The Whiskey Ring involved several layers of corruption. President Lincoln had raised the tax on whiskey immensely, to help pay for the war. The tax collectors were in cahoots with both Republicans and Democrats, keeping money for themselves, and donating to both parties, leaving little for the Treasury. A portion of the whiskey tax was actually used to fund George B. McClellan's run for the presidency against Lincoln in 1864. Grant had appointed John MacDonald as supervisor of the Internal Revenue Service in St. Louis, against the advice of the president's colleagues. Most of the distillers were in the Midwest and went along with Mac-Donald's scheme, saving themselves money by paying less tax and paying a portion of their savings to MacDonald and his associates. For five years the take went on, involving over two hundred people, including Orville Babcock. Eventually the Treasury Department noticed the loss of revenue, and Grant sent Benjamin Bristow, his secretary of the treasury, to investigate.

A shady character himself, Bristow had made money by wartime profiteering, though Grant was unaware of it. Bristow smeared the reputation of a Treasury Department architect, who resigned; Bristow then spread word that he had fired the man for corruption. Bristow set himself up as a reformer and had presidential ambitions.

Bristow planned to transfer all the revenue agents, which would have broken up the Whiskey Ring, but MacDonald raced to Washington and persuaded the president that it was a bad idea. Bristow canceled the transfers, but even so he recovered over $3 million in whiskey taxes and brought charges against 238 perpetrators, including Grant's brother Orvil, Grant's farm manager, and Julia's brother and brother-in-law as well as Orville Babcock and John MacDonald. Grant announced that there would be no immunity for testifying against higher-ups, which he thought only encouraged perjury. Despite this, of the 238 people indicted, 110 were convicted.

In spite of the evidence against Babcock, Grant continued his loyalty to his secretary. He announced that he would go to St. Louis to testify in Babcock's behalf, but he was finally persuaded not to go in person. He did, however, give a lengthy deposition, stating that if Babcock were guilty, he, Grant, would have known of it. Babcock was acquitted. Grant took him back as his secretary, but most people considered him guilty, a reflection on the administration.

Soon Babcock was indicted again, for swindles committed two years earlier in his job as superintendent of public buildings. Again he was acquitted, but it was clear that he had to go. He was appointed to a third job, inspector of lighthouses, away from Washington, D.C. He drowned when his boat overturned in Florida on his way to Mosquito Inlet Lighthouse.

Grant almost always made a mistake when he put a former army buddy in charge of a branch of government. Another such

U.S. District Court in St. Louis, where Grant's secretary Orville Babcock and over a hundred others were tried for their part in the Whiskey Ring.
LIBRARY OF CONGRESS

mistake was appointing William Belknap as secretary of war. The War Department then handled Indian affairs. Belknap lived high and needed money. His wife persuaded him to appoint a friend of hers to the military trading post at Fort Sill in Indian Territory. In return, Belknap would receive a split of the profits. When his wife died, Belknap married her equally voracious younger sister, who continued the arrangement. People began to question how the Belknaps could live so well on his $8,000 annual salary. The answer soon came, and the House of Representatives began to plan impeachment. Moments before the vote, Grant called Belknap to his office and demanded his resignation. Belknap reluctantly agreed, saving himself from impeachment. Frustrated, the House of Representatives was never able to punish him for anything.

Grant refused a third term as president, although Julia declared that she loved the White House and wanted to stay on. It had been their home longer than any other place. Their children had grown up there, and their daughter Nellie had married there.

After the disputed election of 1876 was settled in favor of Rutherford Hayes, Grant arranged for the incoming president to be sworn in secretly two days early.

The Grants were free to travel. He had saved nothing during his two terms as president; the expenses of entertaining had taken more than his salary. However, he had been given what was thought at the time to be worthless shares in a mining company in Nevada. It was the Comstock Lode, and by 1877 his shares were worth $25,000. He sold them and the family set off around the world. They first visited Nellie and her husband, Algernon Sartoris, in England, then went on to tour Europe, Egypt, Palestine, Turkey, India, Siam, Hong Kong, China, and Japan, returning to America two years after they'd left.

Although Grant had expressed no wish to run for a third term as president, friends put his name forward at the convention in 1880. He failed to get enough votes for the nomination. He was made president of the Mexican Southern Railroad, which had its headquarters in New York, and did all he could to see Mexico develop economically. His friends bought him a house in Manhattan so he could live close to his new job.

He was never free of money worries. His son Ulysses Grant Jr., called "Buck," who had graduated from Harvard and from Columbia Law School, joined what he thought was an investment firm along with Ferdinand Ward. The former president sold his property in St. Louis and invested it with the firm, but Ward was a swindler, running a Ponzi scheme.

Eventually the truth came out that the firm was collapsing. Grant borrowed $150,000 from William H. Vanderbilt, attempting to save his son's honor, but it was "too little, too late." The firm owed $16 million and had a little over $50,000 in assets. Vanderbilt offered to forgive the debt, but Julia refused the offer. Instead, Vanderbilt took the military memorabilia the Grants had, sold part of the collection, and returned the rest to the former general.

In 1885 Grant was diagnosed with terminal cancer of the esophagus, brought on by years of smoking. What security could he leave Julia? His friends Mark Twain and Walt Whitman, who both admired his writing, urged him to write his memoirs. The previous year he had written four articles for *Century Magazine* at $500 each, and they had been well-received. If he earned money for a book, his creditors would take it all, so he gave the rights to the manuscript to Julia and the sales contract with the publisher was in her name.

While Grant wrote, the publisher's agents crisscrossed the country, selling 150,000 copies before the book was published. As he summoned his last bit of energy to correct the page proofs, Grant knew that the book was a commercial success. It was a literary success as well, depicting the man and the events he lived through and shaped.

To escape the heat of Manhattan in the summer of 1885, he was taken to the home of a friend near Saratoga. Here he died on July 23, 1885. He was one of America's most underrated presidents, but it was due to his own refusal to admit and punish the wrongdoing of others.

SOURCES

My main source was the excellent biography, *Ulysses S. Grant—Soldier & President* by Geoffrey Perret (New York: Modern Library, 1997). For Grant's early life, Edward G. Longacre's *General Ulysses S. Grant, the Soldier & the Man* (Cambridge, Mass.: Da Capo Press, 2007) is a good source. I also consulted Volume 6 of the Time-Life Series, *1861–1876: The Union Restored* by T. Harry Williams (New York: Time-Life, 1963) and *Reconstruction—Political and Economic* by William Archibald Dunning (New York: Harper & Brothers, 1907).

I also referred to the following Web sites:

www.senate.gov/artandhistory/history/minute/War_Secretarys_Impeachment_Trial.htm (accessed April 2, 2010); "The Last High White House Official Indicted While in Office:

U.S. Grant's Orville Babcock," History News Network, http://hnn
.us/articles/17562.html (accessed April 2, 2010); "A Complete and
Graphic Account of the Crédit Mobilier Investigation," Central
Pacific Railroad Photographic History Museum Web site, http://
cprr.org/Museum/Credit_Mobilier_1873.html (accessed April 2,
2010); "Orville E. Babcock," Wikipedia, www.wikipedia.org/wiki
/Orville_E._Babcock, and "Whiskey Ring," Wikipedia, www
.wikipedia.org/wiki/Whiskey_Ring (both accessed March 28, 2010).

CHAPTER ELEVEN

The Disputed Election

Jerks don't always show up as single individuals. Sometimes whole groups can be jerks, when their political beliefs and desire for control leads them to dishonesty and corruption. An example of this is the Election of 1876.

In the midst of celebrating America's one-hundredth birthday in 1876, a campaign was going on to decide who would be the next president. Republican Rutherford B. Hayes, the governor of Ohio, ran against Democrat Samuel Tilden, the reform governor of New York. This election, while much of the South still seethed under the military rule of Reconstruction, is considered the most corrupt presidential contest ever held in the United States. A president was chosen only two days before the scheduled inauguration date, March 4, but there was no winner. Both candidates and their supporters came away looking like crooks.

The Republicans were accused of making a deal with three former Confederate states, and the Democrats were accused of intimidating freed slaves at the ballot box. There were villains on both sides—including Dan Sickles, who had already committed a series of misdeeds—and there was more than enough blame to go around.

The day after the election, in headlines that would be echoed for another New York presidential candidate, Thomas Dewey, in 1948, newspapers declared Tilden the winner, with a plurality of the popular votes. But the United States chooses its presidents and vice presidents by the Electoral College vote not the popular vote, and Tilden had 184 electoral votes, one short of the majority needed for election. The votes from Florida, Louisiana, South Carolina, and Oregon were uncertain.

For five months Americans didn't know who would succeed to the highest office, and in the end victory went to the Republican

Samuel Tilden is sobbing, "Ruthy Hayes got my Presidency and won't give it back."
RUTHERFORD HAYES PRESIDENTIAL CENTER

candidate. Critics were quick to accuse the Republicans, for this election came on the heels of the corruption rife in the Grant administration.

Many Republicans were as critical of their party as the Democrats were. As Congressman George Julian of Indiana said, the Republican Party had been formed for lofty aims: to make sure that slavery did not spread into the territories and to free those already enslaved. The party had achieved both those aims, but it had turned vindictive in its punishment of the South, had abandoned the freed and vulnerable blacks, and had lost its soul in pursuit of money. He thought that the party might as well be abandoned and another formed to face the problems of 1876.

America in 1876 was a much-changed nation from the fragile colonies that declared their independence in 1776. The continent had been claimed all the way to the Pacific Ocean, its northern and southern boundaries were settled with Canada and Mexico, its vast expanse crossed by the transcontinental railroad. Its ships carried on a world trade, and its ambassadors had been sent to far-flung countries. Gold and silver had been discovered throughout the West, oil had been found in Pennsylvania and Ohio, and coal, timber, and iron ore were plentiful. Immigrants poured into its cities, eager to benefit from the nation's fabled riches.

But there were problems. America's riches were poorly distributed. While the super-rich built mansions and traveled in their own private rail cars, the poor were often crowded into filthy tenements, sending their children as young as six years of age to work in factories. A recession had begun in 1873, putting one in four workers out of a job. Settlers still battled Indians in the West. In fact, General George Custer and more than 250 of his troops would lose their lives in Montana on June 25, 1876, just months before the disputed election. Women, no matter how wealthy or well educated, could not vote.

The South especially suffered. One of its main sources of wealth, slaves, had been freed. Unused to supporting themselves, they soon reverted to a situation close to slavery, working as sharecroppers for their former owners. The Freedmen's Bureau, set up to educate them, gradually faded away. Property owners lost their land to taxes, and former Southern leaders had been stripped of their civil rights; the last few Confederate officers were not given back the right to vote until 1898.

So, despite the celebrations of the Centennial and the wonders on display at Philadelphia, the United States was a troubled country, yearning for change.

Both candidates for president were considered honest men who could bring reform to America.

Rutherford Hayes was the three-time governor of Ohio and a former U.S. congressman from that state. He was called a "sure-footed politician" and was said to have "the Hayes luck." He had served in the Union army during the Civil War and been wounded, and campaigns often "waved the bloody shirt," reminding voters of the war. When he won election as governor for the third time, he wrote in his diary that he expected he would be asked to run for the presidency, a prediction that proved accurate. Republican leaders called on him, asking him to declare his candidacy.

As convention time approached, however, his nomination was not a sure thing. Also hoping to be nominated were Benjamin Bristow of Kentucky, Senator Roscoe Conkling of New York, and Senator James G. Blaine of Maine. Bristow was a reformer, who, although he had prosecuted members of the Whiskey Ring, had a shady past of his own. Both Bristow and Hayes supported civil service reform. However, Bristow was a Southerner and lacked the support of many Northern voters. Conkling, a product of the Boss Tweed political machine of New York City, opposed any kind of reform. Blaine, despite his involvement in a railroad scandal, was the party favorite.

The one candidate they did not want was Ulysses Grant running for a third term. The House of Representatives even passed a resolution to that effect.

After the Republican convention in Cincinnati, the Louisville *Courier-Journal* described the nominating process as a horse race, with Hayes, the "Ohio colt," coming up to the finish line and passing the other entrants at just the right time. Hayes won with 384 votes to Blaine's 351.

In St. Louis, the Democrats nominated the New York governor, Samuel Tilden, who, though he had become wealthy as a corporate lawyer, had played a leading role in disbanding the Boss Tweed ring. For the first time since before the Civil War, the Democrats had control of the U.S. House of Representatives, and they thought that with Tilden in the White House, they could undo much of the corruption and excess of the Radical Republicans. Moreover, since Tilden came from the state with the most electoral votes, he began with an edge over Hayes.

Hayes also thought that he could reform the government. He pointed out that the Republicans had made mistakes during the tumult of war and its aftermath, but they had done good things too. They had granted the right to vote to over four million former slaves, they had successfully brought the Union back together, and they had made a beginning in paying down the huge national debt. Mark Twain supported Hayes, especially for his stand on reforming the civil service. Twain thought the United States had done a good job of training and promoting its military according to their ability but had filled the civil service offices with "ignoramuses," whose only qualification was party loyalty.

The two presidential candidates pretty much stayed above the fray, but their supporters did not. Tilden, a bachelor, was depicted in cartoons wearing a dress and pursuing male voters. Hayes was accused of stealing $1,000 given to him for safekeeping by a soldier who was later killed. Records showed that the soldier had never had any money, but the smear made the rounds with voters.

Voter intimidation was widespread in the South, especially against blacks. In Florida, sharecroppers, who usually ran up debts until the crops were harvested, were told that if they voted Republican, a 25 percent surcharge would be added to their bills. One Democrat-leaning railroad passed out numbered ballots to its employees, with the warning that they "had better show up on election day." Another railroad, Republican-dominated, threatened to fire any worker who voted Democrat. A Democrat railroad superintendent sent a crew of black workers northward to repair tracks. Their engine conveniently broke down, and they were unable to return to vote.

Louisiana had the most election-related violence, including several murders. Republicans had taken black voters for granted, but controlled the "returning board," those who would report the election results, so they did little campaigning. However, several black men were killed, and their murders were never solved.

In South Carolina, despite the peacemaking efforts of gubernatorial candidate Wade Hampton, biracial riots broke out in several places, including Charleston.

On Election Day, November 7, 1876, about eight million votes were cast. As the returns poured in to the national headquarters of the Republican Party in New York, it soon became clear that Tilden had won by a quarter-million more votes than Hayes. According to some reports, the electoral votes were skewed by the actions of Dan Sickles, the former Democratic congressman and Union general, now a Republican. He later claimed that he took it upon himself to send telegrams to the governors of Louisiana, Florida, and South Carolina, asking them to make sure their electoral votes remained committed to Hayes. With the electoral votes from those three states and Oregon, Hayes would have one more vote than Tilden, 185 to 184, and would be elected. The Republican editor of the *New York Times* and lobbyist William Chandler sent similar telegrams later that same evening. They went Sickles one better, also sending telegrams to Oregon and California.

When the popular vote results were published the following day, Hayes conceded the election and Tilden celebrated, claiming that while he had attracted many Republican votes, he had not expected such a large electoral majority, 206 to 133 for Hayes. The New York *World* claimed that the Democrats had thrown off sixteen years of corrupt Republican rule. The *Times* said that the results were "in doubt," as three Southern states were likely to go

Republican. Two days later other newspapers retracted their victory stories and indicated that the election was "in dispute." The *World* stated that Tilden had won all three of the Southern states in question.

President Grant sent federal troops to the three states— South Carolina, Florida, and Louisiana—to maintain order and to ensure that the ballots were handled and counted carefully. Three days after the election, South Carolina chose a five-man board to decide if the state's votes should go to Hayes or Tilden. All five were Republican, and not surprisingly, they awarded the votes to Hayes. They also disqualified the votes from two counties on the grounds of fraud, and there probably was fraud. South Carolina had no voter registration law, so residents could vote repeatedly, and nonresidents or even non-citizens could vote. Hayes had more popular votes than Tilden by the first count. However, despite the Republican's presidential vote victory in South Carolina, a Democrat and former Confederate officer, Wade Hampton, was elected governor. Democrats and Republicans accused each other of cheating.

Louisiana went for Tilden by several thousand votes. When the Election Board examined the ballots, they threw out 15,000 as fraudulent, 13,000 of them cast for Tilden. Observers felt that if there had been no fraud, Hayes would have won cleanly, as most blacks voted Republican, and Louisiana had more eligible black voters than whites.

Florida had four electoral votes. Observers reported fraud here as well, with more votes cast in some districts than there were residents. Again, the fault lay partly with the state's loose voter registration rules, which allowed voters to cast their ballots wherever they wished. One observer, General Lew Wallace, soon to be the author of *Ben-Hur*, wrote that there was fraud by both parties, as well as violence. No matter which candidate won, he had won illegally.

Both sides sent observers, called "visiting statesmen," to make sure the votes were correctly tallied, certified, and reported. And, despite Tilden's protest, his nephew attempted to bribe electors to influence the results.

The three Southern states had a total of 19 electoral votes. Each state had two sets of electors. The Democratic electors planned to cast the states' votes for Tilden while the Republican electors would cast the entire set of votes for Hayes.

If all the disputed Southern electoral votes went to Hayes, the election would still go to Tilden. Oregon, still in dispute, had three electors, all Republican. However, one of the three worked for the post office and as a federal officeholder was disqualified from being an elector. Officially, voters cast their votes not for the presidential candidates, but for electors who would then choose the winner. The Democratic governor of Oregon seized the opportunity to eliminate the Republican elector and appointed a Democrat to fill that position, but the Oregon secretary of state gave certificates to all three Republicans. This one vote for Tilden would have given him the election even if all the disputed Southern electoral votes were awarded to Hayes.

How was the election to be decided? According to the Constitution, the president of the Senate—the vice president of the United States—is to open the box of ballots cast by the Electoral College and count them in the presence of the senators and members of the House of Representatives. Republicans controlled the Senate, so Democrats refused to have the Senate president decide on the validity of ballots.

The Constitution further states that in case of a tie, the House of Representatives will vote, with each state having one vote. Since the House was controlled by Democrats, the Republicans did not want this procedure to happen. Moreover, the election was not a tie in the usual sense. Things were merely at an impasse.

The Senate and House met in January 1877 and agreed to set up an Electoral Commission to decide the validity of ballots in the four disputed states. It would have five senators (three Republican, two Democrat), five members of the House (three Democrats and two Republicans), and five Supreme Court justices. There were two Republican justices and two Democrats. It was assumed that the fifth one would be Justice David Davis, an independent. He was regarded as fair and was expected to award the disputed votes to Tilden, who had won the most popular votes.

Then unexpectedly, the Illinois legislature elected Davis to the Senate. (Senators at this time were not popularly elected but were chosen by the legislature of their state.) The Democrats claimed it was a Republican trick to keep him off the commission, but no Republicans in the Illinois legislature had voted for him. The Republicans claimed it was a Democratic trick, since Davis was clearly a Democrat and would not have to resign from the court to take his Senate seat until after the commission had met.

Davis himself settled the matter by announcing that he would not accept appointment to the Electoral Commission, as it would open him to criticism. Following his announcement, Associate Justice Joseph Bradley was chosen for the commission. Although he was a Republican, he was acceptable to the Democrats, who considered him also a fair-minded man.

The night before a decision was to be announced on the Florida ballots, Justice Bradley was visited by a Democratic friend, who was told that Bradley had written his opinion favoring Tilden. However, Bradley had a series of other visitors that night, and when the commission met in the morning, he announced his decision in favor of Hayes. Tilden later claimed that one of the justices—presumed to be Bradley—had offered to sell his vote for $200,000. There was also a suggestion that representatives from the Texas and Pacific Railroad had influenced Bradley. Bradley denied that anyone had influenced him or that he had privately discussed the decision. Was Bradley the man responsible for stealing an election?

For determining the validity of the ballots from Florida, Louisiana, and South Carolina, voting by the commission was strictly along party lines: eight to seven.

What about the questionable Oregon delegate? The commission accepted the three Republicans who had certificates, even if one should probably have been disqualified.

Hayes was thus certified as president.

Democrats in the House of Representatives decided to filibuster rather than accept the results of the Electoral Commission, but when the matter came to a vote, they discovered that Southern Democrats had accepted the commission's report. It was said that the businessmen of America, especially Southerners, wanted "quiet" more than they wanted Tilden.

The Northern House Democrats suspected that a deal had been made behind the scenes. One possibility was that Tom Scott, who hoped to get federal money for internal improvements in the South—in particular, for the Texas and Pacific Railroad—had brokered such a deal. With a Democratic president and a Democratic House, his chances would have been slim. With a Republican president and Senate, there was a good possibility that he could get at least some of the money he wanted.

On February 26, a group of Democrats and Republicans, from North and South, had met at the Wormley Hotel in Washington to work out the real "deal" that resolved the disputed election. Hayes agreed to remove the last of the federal troops from the conquered South and to appoint at least one Southerner to his Cabinet. In return, the Democratic governor-elect of Louisiana agreed to treat Republicans and blacks in his state fairly, and Democrats in the House agreed to lift the filibuster and to support James Garfield, a Republican from Hayes's state of Ohio, as speaker of the House.

Hayes was inaugurated as president, not once but twice. There was still so much unrest in the country that his supporters feared that chaos, and perhaps even an outbreak of war, might prevent his being sworn in. So he secretly took the oath of office in the White House as Grant's guest on March 3. Then on March 5, 1877, he publicly became the president, thus ending the longest-disputed election in American history.

Democrat newspapers published editions edged in black, and Hayes was referred to as "Rutherfraud" and "His Fraudulency." Outrage against him died down somewhat when telegrams emerged showing that Tilden's nephew, William Pelton, had attempted to bribe Southern returning committees.

Hayes did have federal troops removed from the former Confederacy, thus ending Reconstruction, and he appointed a Southerner as postmaster general. This was considered the "plum" appointment of the government, as the postmaster general could and did appoint many people to jobs as postmasters and mail carriers. Hayes did not, however, support funds for the Texas and Pacific Railroad, to the disappointment of Tom Scott.

And Tilden? His supporters urged him to sue, taking his case to the Supreme Court, but he declined. He would return

After the disputed election of 1876, both parties were accused of fraud, but the Republicans were most criticized. The GOP elephant says, "Another such victory and I am undone."
GOOGLEIMAGES

to private life and his lucrative law practice, he said, secure in the knowledge that he had been elected to the highest office in the land, without having to assume any of its responsibilities.

Rutherford B. Hayes was a one-term president as he had promised to be when he accepted the nomination. He and his wife—called "Lemonade Lucy" for her refusal to allow alcohol in the White House—and their large family were popular.

History has a way of resolving bad situations, and however the election was conducted, Hayes was probably the better choice. Tilden had Parkinson's disease, and his health continued to decline. Given the stresses of the presidency, he might have died in office.

In 1880 House Speaker James A. Garfield was elected president, only to be assassinated soon after taking office. Chester A. Arthur, who had been part of the New York political machine, became president.

In 1884 the Democrats finally took control of the White House, electing Grover Cleveland as president. Thus ended the longest political control in America by one party.

SOURCES

America in 1876: The Way We Were by Lally Weymouth (New York: Random House, 1976) gave me valuable background information, as did Kenneth Stampp's *The Era of Reconstruction, 1865–1877* (New York: Alfred A. Knopf, 1976) and *Reconstruction: After the Civil War* by John Hope Franklin (Chicago: University of Chicago Press, 1961).

For details of the election, I consulted *Fraud of the Century: Rutherford B. Hayes, Samuel Tilden and the Stolen Election of 1876* by Roy Morris Jr. (New York: Simon & Schuster, 2003) and *Centennial Crisis—The Disputed Election of 1876* by Supreme Court Justice William H. Rehnquist (New York: Random House, 2004).

I also read the extensive biography, *Rutherford B. Hayes, Warrior and President* by Ari Hoogenboom (Lawrence: University of Kansas Press, 1995).

CHAPTER TWELVE

The Despicable Despoiler:
W. C. P. Breckinridge

Aprominent married politician has an affair with a naïve young woman. She becomes pregnant, and he promises to marry her when his wife dies. Sounds very modern, doesn't it? But this affair began in 1884 and ended ten years later with a sensational trial that was covered by scores of newspapers across America and included details so salacious that the presiding judge refused to allow women to hear some of them.

The congressman was William Campbell Preston Breckinridge of Kentucky, member of a distinguished family that included a vice president of the United States who also ran against Lincoln in the 1860 election. The congressman was named for General William Campbell, a Revolutionary War hero, and had himself served as a captain in the Confederate army. He was a Mason and a member of the Knights Templar.

Congressman Breckinridge, born in Baltimore in 1837, had twice been married by 1884 and was the father of five children. He was known as a womanizer, enjoying women of various races and reputations, and was on a first-name basis with the owner of a brothel in Lexington, Kentucky, referred to as a "house of assignation."

He had been elected to Congress but had not yet taken office when he met Madeline Pollard. She was seventeen, on her way home by train to Frankfort, Kentucky, from Wesleyan Academy in Cincinnati, summoned by her mother to help care for her dying sister.

Breckinridge was returning from a business trip in Cincinnati. He sat down in the same compartment with young Madeline and used one of the oldest lines around: "You look familiar. Don't I know you?"

Madeline Pollard slumps to the table, sobbing, during the trial of her breach of promise lawsuit against Congressman W.C.P. Breckinridge.

Madeline responded that he wouldn't know her but that she knew who he was and that her father had admired his cousin John Breckinridge. The congressman-elect asked if he might call on her. She answered primly and properly that she was sure her mother and sister would be glad to receive him but that at the moment her sister was very ill.

The two went their separate ways at journey's end, but their meeting would have far-reaching consequences.

Madeline was the poor daughter of a saddle maker who had died when she was ten. Her father, also a Mason, had been well-read and pushed his children to get an education. Lacking money for schooling, Madeline made an agreement with a neighbor, James Rhodes (in some articles spelled Rodes), who was almost fifty, that if he would finance her education, she would either pay him back or marry him. She planned to become a teacher and repay him. He pushed her to quit school and marry him, as time was running out for him to have a family.

Madeline didn't want to marry and wrote to Breckinridge to ask if he, as a lawyer, could advise her on whether she could get out of the contract or whether she must marry Rhodes. On his next trip to Cincinnati, Breckinridge called at the academy, and when Madeline came to the parlor to meet him, he said that he could not talk freely about her business, which he presumed she wished to keep private from her classmates. He suggested taking her to a concert that night, if she could get permission to go with him. She said the rules were more relaxed since it was summer—she was in summer school making up for the class time she had missed while caring for her sister. Breckinridge told the chaperones that he was a friend of her father's.

He arrived that evening in a closed carriage, and soon after they drove away from the campus, he began to make advances. When she protested, he told her she was being foolish and prud-ish but took her back to school. She agreed to meet him at the library the next day, where they could talk about her contract with Rhodes.

At the library, Breckinridge said he could only talk in whispers because of the rules of quiet and said a friend had a home nearby where they could have some privacy. They went by streetcar to the house, where he showed her into a small parlor. A woman greeted them and said the upstairs room would be ready soon. When Madeline refused to go upstairs, Breckinridge locked her in the parlor. Eventually he let her out and took her back to her dormitory, saying charming things all the way.

Madeline should have been horrified and repulsed by this married rogue thirty years her senior, but as she testified later, he was fascinating and seductive. She fell under his spell. He urged her to transfer to Sayre Institute in Lexington, so they could be together frequently. He said he would help her get a teaching job so she could repay Rhodes. In the meantime, he wanted her to meet him in Lexington for the weekend. He sent a telegram, signing it from her mother, summoning her home.

They spent the weekend together, when, as Madeline later testified, "He accomplished my seduction and my ruin." They began to meet frequently, and Madeline became pregnant. She stayed in school at Sayre until her condition began to show, then went to Cincinnati where she had the baby at Foundling Hospital run by the Black Cap Sisters of Charity. She used the name Louise Wilson. She wanted to keep her baby and go somewhere she was not known, but Breckinridge told her she must give up the child. He would marry her after his wife died, but if she had the child, people would know it was his.

Madeline was seriously ill after childbirth, probably of peritonitis. Breckinridge helped her write a series of letters to her mother, dated at intervals, to cover her absence. These he mailed from railway mail cars, so there would be no postmark.

Madeline returned to Sayre for two more years of schooling, all the while seeing Breckinridge whenever he was in Kentucky. In 1887 she became pregnant again. He asked her to move to Washington, which she did. She stayed first in a boardinghouse as "Mrs. Foster." Breckinridge called on her, as "Mr. Foster," but he was recognized and she had to move. She stayed briefly at St. Ann's Foundling Asylum and then lived with a midwife until the baby was born in February 1888. Breckinridge paid all her bills, including funeral expenses for the baby, who died two months later.

Afterward, he helped Madeline get a government job, but she lost it when she made an unfortunate remark about a congressman. She lived at a convent for over two years and also spent a short time in Cambridge, Massachusetts, and a summer at Bread Loaf, Vermont, at a writers conference.

In July 1892, Breckinridge's wife died. He told Madeline that he must wait a year to remarry, out of respect to convention. That fall, Madeline, intelligent except where Breckinridge was concerned, was given the opportunity to study in Berlin, Germany. Breckinridge begged her to stay in Washington, saying he couldn't bear to be without her, and she turned down the scholarship.

Breckinridge introduced Madeline to Mrs. Luke Blackburn, widow of the former governor of Kentucky and a "proper gentlewoman," asking her to take Madeline "under her wing" and see to it that she was equipped for her place in society. He told Mrs. Blackburn that he and Madeline were engaged.

By March 1893, Madeline was pregnant again. She and Breckinridge visited Mrs. Blackburn on Good Friday and told her they planned to be married soon, although Mrs. Blackburn said she'd urged Madeline to give him up. Breckinridge said that rumors he was planning to marry Mrs. Louisa Scott Wing, a widowed relative, were untrue, but he added that the rumors of his remarriage would help his adult children reconcile to the idea that he would eventually remarry.

On a trip to New York that month, Breckinridge spent twelve days with Mrs. Wing, and on April 29, married her in a secret ceremony. Breckinridge asked the justice of the peace to keep the marriage a secret for three months.

Madeline, relying on his promise to marry her, had their engagement announced. He issued a denial.

He sent for Madeline to join him in New York, having her registered at his hotel as his daughter. She took along a pistol, and when she showed it to him and claimed she would shoot him and herself if he didn't marry her, he took it away. He left her alone for the weekend, telling her he had business appointments. He was involved with a company that wanted to send him abroad with $30 million to start a railroad, he claimed. While Breckinridge was gone, she called the men whose names he'd mentioned and discovered he'd lied. It was just one of many lies he had told and would tell the gullible Madeline. Furious, she found the gun and confronted him when he returned. Charming as ever, he convinced her that she was wrong and sent for Mrs. Blackburn to accompany her back to Washington. He sent flowers and a note, again promising marriage.

On May 17, Breckinridge took Madeline before the Washington chief of police, Major William Moore, claiming that Madeline had threatened his life. Madeline told the policeman the whole story, admitting she'd wanted to kill Breckinridge if he wouldn't marry her. In the presence of Moore, Breckinridge repeated that he planned to marry Madeline on May 31, though they had discussed waiting until after the baby's birth and though he well knew that he was already married. Moore took the pistol from Madeline, lectured her briefly on being careful of her conduct, and advised her not to carry a weapon.

On May 24, Madeline had a miscarriage.

She wrote to Breckinridge by registered mail requesting that he reiterate his promise to marry her. "If you fail to answer and confirm," she wrote, " . . . I will seek redress."

He did not answer. He had always been able to control or cajole her. Not this time. On August 12, 1893, she filed suit against him for $50,000 for breach of promise. She charged seduction, illegitimate parentage, and nine years of duplicity. Prominent attorneys Calderon Carlisle and Jeremiah Wilson filed the suit on her behalf.

The suit stated, "Plaintiff, Madeline Valeria Pollard, sues the defendant and states that about the first of April 1884, she was a maiden of seventeen years and was a student at Wesleyan Female

Seminary in the city of Cincinnati, and the defendant, being a married man of 47 years of age and a distinguished lawyer and orator, who was known only by sight to her, he made her acquaintance by accosting her on a railroad train which she was traveling on from school to Frankfort, Kentucky on account of the grievous illness of her sister." It went on to detail their affair.

The morning the suit was filed, Breckinridge went to Philadelphia for the launch of the steamer *Minneapolis*. On his return reporters questioned him. He responded that it was "vexatious, vindictive blackmail" and, sounding very modern, added that he would say no more until he had talked to his lawyers.

Breckinridge waited until fifteen minutes before the deadline before filing an answer on September 23. He denied everything. Miss Pollard had accosted him on the train, he said, and she was then over twenty. He said when she'd asked his advice about her engagement, he'd advised her to marry Rhodes. He'd never seduced her or made her pregnant, and of course he had never promised to marry her.

The story hit newspapers across America, with most taking Madeline's side. This was a sensational story. A congressman, a married man involved in a lurid affair! Representatives should be above reproach, editorials opined, urging him to resign until he cleared himself. Breckinridge was put under police protection, fearing Madeline's brother would beat him.

Before the trial began, Breckinridge and his attorneys set out to destroy Madeline's reputation. She had admitted to the nine-year affair and only asked that Breckinridge admit his share of guilt. Instead, he bullied and paid witnesses who claimed that Madeline was much older than she said, that she had had affairs with others, that she had lived and worked in a brothel. He claimed that he had been helpless to resist the seductions of such an experienced, evil woman.

He even prevented notaries in Lexington from taking depositions of Madeline's witnesses. This tactic, however, was to backfire, as it meant bringing the witnesses to Washington to testify.

How could Madeline hope to win against a powerful, ruthless congressman? How could she pay for the services of high-priced lawyers and the cost of bringing witnesses from Kentucky? She had no money and was living at the Episcopal House of Mercy.

Mrs. Blackburn came to her rescue, writing letters to friends to solicit funds for Madeline's defense. Money trickled in, in small and large amounts, and women's rights groups chipped in. Each lawyer's fee was $4,000, and the typing bill for depositions was $800, in addition to travel expenses.

Breckinridge had his own high-priced lawyers, including Breckinridge's son Desha, Benjamin Butterworth, and William Mattingly, as well as three other lawyers. Presiding over the trial was Judge Andrew Bradley. The twelve jurors were all white men. Eight possible jurors had been rejected, including five black men. Women were not allowed to be on juries.

Both sides said there was no possibility of compromise, so the trial began.

Madeline arrived in court each day dressed all in black and accompanied by one of the Sisters of Mercy.

Among Madeline's first two witnesses were Mrs. Blackburn and Police Chief Moore, who both testified that in their presence Congressman Breckinridge had stated that he intended to marry Madeline. The chief further testified that Breckinridge had sent him letters urging him to prevent Madeline from damaging her reputation by going ahead with the lawsuit. He also said that two of Breckinridge's friends had come to him with money to "help Madeline."

A former classmate testified that Madeline had been only seventeen and innocent when she met Breckinridge. The midwife who delivered the second baby testified that Breckinridge had paid her bill.

Sarah Gess, an African-American woman, was one of the witnesses whose depositions could not be taken in Kentucky, so she was brought to Washington to testify in person for Madeline. She said that she ran a "house of assignation," that Breckinridge had brought Madeline there about fifty times over eight years, and that she had seen him kissing Madeline. She added that Madeline had never been there with any other man.

Madeline testified that her relationship with Breckinridge had gone on for eight years, until May 17, 1893. "All this time we continued this miserable sin and never for a moment was there any suggestion that it should cease, until he finally left me without giving any reason or excuse for doing so," she stated.

She said that she had broken her engagement with Rhodes in December 1884, in the presence of Breckinridge, when she was pregnant. By this time she had fallen totally in love with Breckinridge and had decided to give herself to him "body and soul, for life."

"Did Rhodes know you were pregnant?" the defense attorney asked.

"Indeed he did not. Otherwise Mr. Breckinridge would not be living today."

Guided by his defense lawyer, Breckinridge claimed that Madeline never told him about any children by him—though he admitted they had had sex relations, occasionally several times a day. He'd had no idea about the children until the suit was filed! What a surprise! He said she had left Lexington in February 1886 without telling him that she was leaving and later had pursued him to Washington. "I did everything I could to prevent her, and to prevent an open breach and scandal." He denied taking Madeline to Sarah Gess's house. The owner of the "house of assignation" had confused him with someone else—all fifty times.

The defense further claimed that Madeline had been engaged five times before she met Breckinridge, and brought forth a fifty-four-year-old carpenter who said that he'd fallen in love with her, proposed, and been engaged for six weeks but that she'd broken the engagement when he couldn't afford a European trip for her. Dr. T. M. Lewis testified that the late A. M. Swope, a collector for the Internal Revenue Service, had fathered Madeline's first baby and that he had tried to get Lewis to perform an abortion.

Since Swope was deceased and could not be cross-examined, Lewis's testimony was ruled hearsay. In addition, Swope's sisters testified that he had been in Europe at the time and never knew Madeline Pollard.

On cross-examination, Breckinridge let his prejudices and his contempt show plainly.

Breckinridge denied writing the letters to Madeline and to her mother, though the judge showed that he had used a typist at the Capitol. Breckinridge also admitted that his home in Lexington was near Sarah Gess's and that he had been there with other women. Breckinridge stated that when he went to Wesleyan Academy to give Madeline advice about Rhodes, she told him she'd had intercourse with Rhodes and he'd told her she could not afford not to marry him. He said he told her that no man could be expected to marry a woman he'd had intercourse with unless he'd seduced her.

Madeline's lawyer then pinned Breckinridge: "And that same rule would apply to a man under the same circumstances?"

In summary, the defense said, Breckinridge was "no worse than the rest of us only he has been discovered."

The jury found that Breckinridge was guilty of breach of promise and awarded Madeline $15,000, not what she had asked for, but still, more than she would ever get from Breckinridge. He, like many other former Confederates, owned no property and had always lived to the extent of his income. His new wife had money, but she would not be expected to pay his penalty.

Breckinridge immediately asked for a new trial but was denied.

Judge Bradley stated to the press, "The plaintiff did not spare herself or attempt to explain or excuse her wicked conduct. She was not claiming to be innocent, only that he was equally guilty. She could have destroyed his career at any time, but did not until he left her no other course."

Madeline thanked her many supporters. She said she had been asked by publishers to edit the trial report for a book and had been asked to go on stage or present a lecture series, but she intended to withdraw from the public eye.

Breckinridge was denounced. Churches demanded that he be expelled from Congress. The Women's Rescue League of Boston asked the people of Kentucky to send him to a "private life of obscurity and oblivion."

The Masons denounced him, as blasphemy, drunkenness, and the violation of women are Masonic offenses. Breckinridge's offense was worse since Madeline was the daughter of a Mason. Breckinridge was "coldly received" in the House of Representatives, and friends attempted to collect money enough to pay his penalty so he would be able to be reelected, but whatever amount was raised, none of it went to Madeline.

A bill was passed to make seduction punishable in Washington. The suit had shown that while breach of promise was on the books, seduction was not.

Not long after the trial, a young woman writing as "Agnes Parker" revealed that Breckinridge's lawyers had hired her to spy on Madeline. She had applied to live at the House of Mercy, pretending to be a "fallen woman," and had been accepted. She had wormed her way into Madeline's confidence and reported regularly to the lawyers. Apparently Madeline had revealed nothing of consequence to the trial. "Agnes Parker" wrote a vitriolic book about Madeline, published as *The Real Madeline Pollard: A Diary of Ten Weeks Association with the Plaintiff in the Famous Breckinridge-Pollard Suit.* The 336-page book soon dropped from sight.

Congressman Breckinridge was defeated for Congress and was not appointed to a desired Senate seat. Every newspaper article about him always connected him to Madeline Pollard, including his obituary when he died in November 1904 after a stroke.

In 1895 he went on a lecture tour, and Madeline's lawyers attempted to get the gate receipts, but the tour paid so little that expenses were barely covered.

Madeline continued to be something of a celebrity. A racehorse was named for her and seems to have run well, though never taking any of the big prizes. Gossipy items appeared about her: One stated that she was asked to go on the lecture tour with Breckinridge, but declined. In September 1894, "Footlight Flashes" noted that "the manager of Madeline Pollard is not overwhelmed with applications for dates for his new star." A month later there was a blurb that she would "appear in the drama" without noting what drama.

An item on May 2, 1895, indicated that Madeline had sailed from New York as the "companion of a charitable woman who is to make a four year trip around the world."

In 1896, the Sayre Institute closed. Because of the notoriety of the Pollard-Breckinridge affair connected with the school, few parents wanted to send their daughters there, and it went bankrupt.

Madeline did not complete the trip around the world. A small item in the Logansport *Pharos* on June 21, 1897, stated that Madeline Pollard was living in London, studying and planning a literary career.

She would have had much to write about.

Sources

My main source was a transcript of the case, *The Celebrated Case of Colonel W. C. P. Breckinridge and Madeline Pollard*, by Fayette Lexington (a pseudonym), published in Chicago by the Current Events Publishing Company in 1894, the year of the trial. I also found the case covered on the Web site http://law.jrank.org /pages/2709/William-Breckinridge-Breach-Promise-Trial-1894.

There are in addition over one thousand mentions of Madeline Pollard in newspapers of the time (half a dozen of which refer to the horse named in her honor). Here are a few that I read in their entirety: *Decatur Daily Republican*, Decatur, Illinois, March 21, 1894, page 2, "A Man's Perfidy"; *Lowell Sun*, Lowell, Massachusetts, April 16, 1894, p. 6, "Got $15,000"; *New Castle News,* New Castle, Pennsylvania, March 28, 1894, p. 8, "Letters to Rhodes"; *New York Times*, March 29, 1894, p. 2, "Miss Pollard Disparaged";

and *Atlanta Constitution,* Atlanta, Georgia, June 24, 1894, p. 9, "A Girl Spy's Story—Spied on Pollard During Trial."

Notice that Breckinridge had had a stroke appeared in the *New York Times* on September 30, 1904, on page 1. His obituary appeared in papers all over America the day after his death, November 18, 1904, always with mention of the Pollard lawsuit and trial.

Mitchell Palmer's anger at Communist and anarchist bombers led him to break the law he was sworn to enforce.
LIBRARY OF CONGRESS

CHAPTER THIRTEEN

Mitchell Palmer
and the Red Raids

Mitchell Palmer in his avid pursuit of Communists, suspected Communists, and anarchists in 1919, in what is called the "Red Scare," trampled on the rights of thousands. He was urged on in this pursuit by thousands of Americans and by President Woodrow Wilson. In 1914, Wilson had offered Palmer the position of secretary of war. Palmer declined, saying that as a Quaker, he was sworn to peace, and if war came, he would be in the position of planning war strategy. As attorney general, he led a "war" of another kind, against terrorist bombers.

Palmer's anti-Red campaign, during which nearly ten thousand people were arrested, was in many ways a continuation of World War I policies. When war began in Europe, many recent immigrants took sides. Congress quickly passed the Espionage Act, the Sedition Act, and the Alien Deportation Act, all giving the government immense powers over the lives of its people. More than two thousand people were prosecuted under the Espionage Act of 1917, and in 1918 the United States deported 11,625 aliens. Investigations of suspected anarchists were often done in secrecy, and the accused had no right to appeal.

Russian Bolsheviks in 1917 overthrew the tsar and set up a Communist government. After America sent a few troops to the Russian Far East to help the "Whites" (those loyal to the tsar and opposed to the "Reds" or Bolsheviks), American Communists stepped up their protests, claiming America was trying to overthrow the Russian government.

When World War I ended, the world was in turmoil. Wilson had declared that the war would "make the world safe for democracy" and would "end all wars." It did neither. Nor did the protesters want democracy. Some wanted Communism, some socialism, and anarchists opposed all government. Workers demanded higher wages and better working conditions. Wilson ignored the domestic ferment, concentrating instead on getting America to back the League of Nations.

The country exploded in 1919. In January, thirty-five thousand dock workers struck in Seattle, paralyzing the city. Anarchists published *The Blast*, praising strikers and calling for a Communist upheaval in the United States.

Bombings followed.

On April 28, 1919, a bomb was sent to the Seattle mayor, but no one was injured. The next day, a bomb arrived at the home of a former U.S. senator in Atlanta. An employee of his opened it, and her hands were blown off. On April 30, the New York post office discovered thirty-four bombs in the mail, which had been set aside for insufficient postage. None had return addresses. The bombs were addressed to public figures, including John D. Rockefeller, Supreme Court Justice Oliver Wendell Holmes, and newly appointed Attorney General Alexander Mitchell Palmer.

Palmer took no action, but in New York the legislature set up the Committee to Investigate Seditious Activities, under the direction of State Senator Clayton Lusk. The Lusk Committee questioned leftists and made raids on their known meeting places.

On May 1, the traditional day for workers' parades, riots broke out in New York, Boston, Cleveland, and other cities. In Cleveland, more than a hundred protesters were injured by gunfire, and two were killed.

As bad as this was, more terrorist acts were to come.

On the night of June 2, 1919, Palmer and his wife had just left their library and gone up to bed when they heard a thump followed by an explosion that rocked their house and tore off the front of it. Their neighbor across the street, Franklin Delano Roosevelt, ran to see what had happened and had to step over body parts on what was left of the Palmers' porch. Apparently the bomber had tripped, and instead of tossing the bomb against the house and escaping, had blown himself to bits. Scattered in the street around his remains were copies of the Communist pamphlet *Plain Words* and an Italian-English dictionary. A ticket stub was found indicating that he had come to Washington on the train from Baltimore. Later investigation located the train conductor who had issued the ticket to a man who got on in Philadelphia, but the conductor could give no description of the bomber.

Plain Words stated, "The time has come when the social questions' solutions can be delayed no longer; class war is on and cannot cease but with a complete victory for the international proletariat." The pamphlet was printed on distinctive pink paper and was signed, "Anarchistic Fighters."

Palmer was not the only target that night. Bombs were also planted in New York; Pittsburgh; Philadelphia; Cleveland; Newtonville, Massachusetts; and Paterson, New Jersey. The night watchman who found a bomb planted at the home of Judge Charles Nott in New York was blown up, his body parts found as far as a block away, and a woman walking nearby was also killed.

The bomb intended for the home of Mayor Harry Davis of Cleveland failed to explode, as did the one at the Philadelphia home of Judge W. H. S. Thompson. A known radical agitator, Robert Johnson, president of the local branch of the Industrial Workers of the World, was blamed for the Philadelphia bomb. He fired on police detectives who arrested him.

Newspaper editors were vehement in their denunciation of the bombings. Typical was the headline in the June 3 issue of *The Marion Daily Star* of Marion, Ohio (whose editor/publisher, Warren G. Harding, would be the next U.S. president): "Reds Bomb Homes and Start Reign of Terror."

President Wilson commanded Palmer to locate and punish the bombers and end the fear that gripped Americans. Who knew where the next bombs might appear? Wilson told Palmer, "Don't let this be a Red nation."

Palmer was justified in seeking to punish the guilty. After all, he had twice been the intended victim of a bombing, and only luck had saved him in both instances. The problem was in how to solve the crimes.

The bombings were the best carried out plot in American history. There had to be a network of terrorists in each city to plant the bombs, but the fact that they had been set to go off almost simultaneously indicated central planning. Solving the bombings would require finding who was in charge of the planning.

Palmer was as well qualified for the task as any man in America. He had graduated Phi Beta Kappa from Swarthmore College in Pennsylvania in 1891 and the following year began his apprenticeship in law. He represented banks and corporations and moved up through the ranks of the Democratic Party. He was elected to Congress from Pennsylvania in 1908 and won reelection in 1910. In 1911 he accepted the position of Pennsylvania's representative to the Democratic National Committee—"temporarily," though he held the post until 1921. In 1912, he was instrumental in seeing that Pennsylvania's electoral votes went to Woodrow Wilson. In return, he hoped to be named attorney general by the new president. However, Wilson offered him the position of secretary of war, which he declined.

In Congress, Palmer proposed a bill to end child labor in America's mines and factories. It passed the House 232 to 44, but President Wilson thought it was unconstitutional and it died in the Senate. Still friendly with Wilson, Palmer let the president persuade him to run for the Senate in 1914. Palmer lost. He returned to private law practice and continued working for the Democratic National Committee.

When the Germans sank the *Lusitania* and the country cried for war, Palmer defended German actions, declaring that Americans had been warned not to travel on the ship. The whole country should not have to suffer through war because a few had ignored the warnings.

When war came, Wilson appointed him to be the alien property custodian. In that post Palmer was responsible for seizing, administering, and sometimes selling enemy assets. Some of the seized assets were companies that made items necessary for conduct of the war, such as munitions, gas masks, and medicines. These he put under the control of his political friends, and when assets such as factories or mines were sold, his friends knew of the auctions when others did not, and profited. He also seized breweries—not necessary for the war effort, but profitable and German-owned. It was years after the war ended before figures for the money earned by the alien property custodian and his friends were brought out. By this time, other corruption by high government officials eclipsed Palmer's wartime profiteering.

Palmer finally got his wish to be attorney general when the position opened up in 1919 and Wilson nominated him. Palmer's nomination for attorney general was put before the Senate on February 27, 1919, and was so promptly approved that he was sworn in on March 5.

Palmer began his term of office by releasing the 10,000 aliens of German ancestry who had been arrested during World War I and refusing any further cooperation with the American Protective League, which had abused civil rights in its spy-hunting activities. He refused to take any action against strikers and protesters after the initial strikes and bomb threats. He recommended that Eugene V. Debs, the convicted pacifist, be released from prison, but President Wilson adamantly refused to commute the sentence.

After the bombings, Palmer had no choice. He had to act against the terrorists. He called on William "Big Bill" Flynn to head up the Bureau of Investigation in solving the crimes. Flynn, a former New York detective and former head of the Secret Service, was an experienced spy hunter. Flynn and his men quickly arrested known socialists and anarchists, taking them off the street and holding some for deportation without a prior trial.

The first weeks of the investigation were frustrating. A hat found at the scene of the Palmer bombing could not be traced, the Italian-English dictionary was one of thousands published, and no print shops were found to carry the pink paper the pamphlet was printed on. The few clues to the identity of the bombers fizzled out.

Palmer moved slowly against the anarchists. In June he called Flynn and others in charge to a meeting in Washington. Besides preventing the rumored mass attacks predicted for July 4, only two weeks away, he also wanted to permanently remove the Communist threat from America. He formed the General Intelligence Division in the Department of Justice and put the division under the charge of young J. Edgar Hoover. Using membership lists of the Communist Party and Communist Labor Party as well as the Industrial Workers of the World, and mailing lists of socialist and anarchist publications, Hoover assembled an impressive list of dangerous people, most of them resident aliens.

Palmer planned to run for president in 1920, and he thought that breaking up the groups of Reds would gain him the national attention he needed to capture the nomination.

There were riots across America during the summer, but they were racial rather than socialist or Communist. Both blacks and whites were killed. Wilson's solution was to resegregate government departments.

By October, attention had returned to workplace agitation. In Boston, the police went on strike. Steelworkers struck in Gary, Indiana, and were forced back to work by military action, and 394,000 coal miners went out on strike at various mines. Americans feared there would be a paralyzing general strike, or even a revolution. The Congress and President Wilson demanded to know what Palmer was doing to break up what they assumed were Communist-led labor movements. As Palmer later said, "I was shouted at from every editorial sanctum . . . and preached at from every pulpit." The U.S. Senate also censured him for doing nothing.

His solution was a widespread raid on known Communist meeting places.

On November 7, 1919—the second anniversary of the Bolshevik revolution—agents of the Justice Department raided centers where Russian immigrants gathered in New York; Chicago; Detroit; St. Louis; Philadelphia; Newark, New Jersey; Jackson, Michigan; New Haven, Hartford, Waterbury, New Britain, and

Ansonia, Connecticut; and Akron and Youngstown, Ohio. In New York, over two hundred men and boys were arrested at the Russian People's House. In the process some were thrown down a staircase and over thirty were beaten badly enough to need medical attention. Two hundred "alleged radicals," to quote the *Chester Times,* were arrested in Chicago. Over a thousand were arrested in all the raids; many of them were quickly released, especially women. Others were packed into small jails or even hallways, lacking food, water, and toilet facilities, and held incommunicado. They were not allowed to talk with lawyers, and their families had no idea what had happened to them.

Many of those arrested carried Communist Party membership cards but were illiterate and had no idea what the cards said. Others had joined because the meeting halls were a place to study English, listen to music, and meet their fellow immigrants. Of the 211 arrested in New York, only 38 were determined to be dangerous, and they were sent to Ellis Island for detention. They were held on $10,000 bail each.

The Justice Department issued a statement declaring that the Union of Russian Workers had been ready for the revolution, which was to overthrow the American government. "Arms had been accumulated and were seized in last night's raids," the department stated. "The 7,000 members of the organization were prepared to begin operating their own government as soon as the U.S. government had been destroyed, it was learned." The statement did not indicate how this information was "learned," or how many and what kind of arms had been seized.

New York state police began reading through the twenty-five tons of "Red" literature that was seized in the raids, though Palmer indicated that the Justice Department was not limiting itself to Communists but was investigating all groups of anarchist aliens.

Palmer was praised for the raids, but he felt that, while he had averted an uprising, the Communists were still "out there," still dangerous. He determined to stage another raid. But before he could do so, on Armistice Day 1919, workers fired on a victory parade in Centralia, Washington. Two marching soldiers were killed, one of whom had served in the army in Europe, the other in Mexico.

Many of those arrested in the November raids were quickly deported. Deportation was the job of the Labor Department, not the Justice Department, and the commissioner of immigration held hearings for those facing deportation. One such person was Emma Goldman, long an agitator against America. She refused to answer any questions but had earlier stated that as long as she was free she would speak out against the American government.

Emma Goldman, an outspoken anarchist deported as a result of the Palmer Raids.
LIBRARY OF CONGRESS

On December 21, 1919, an old army transport ship set sail from Ellis Island with 249 deportees on board, including Goldman and her lover, Alexander Berkman. Berkman had served fourteen years for attempting to assassinate Henry Clay Frick, manager of a mining company whose workers were on strike.

Since Russia was still at war, the ship headed for Finland. From there, the deportees were taken overland to Russia.

Palmer decided to conduct another raid on January 2, 1920, to net not just hundreds, but thousands of revolutionists. Agents of the Justice Department infiltrated various Communist groups so that they could make sure the members held a meeting on January 2. Palmer had three thousand blank arrest warrants printed, with the names to be filled in as the anarchists were taken into custody. During the raids, all the arrest warrants were used, and an additional two thousand people were arrested without warrants.

Although Palmer was again praised for the raids and arrests, a few people began to question the methods used and the treatment of those arrested, especially as word got out that eight hundred people had been crowded into a corridor in a Detroit post office building, deprived of water and food for twenty-four hours. A federal judge ordered the release of many of those arrested, and dropped most of the charges and reduced the bail for those still held.

The bombing investigations were still ongoing, and some solid evidence was finally uncovered during a raid of the print shop of an Italian radical paper. Agents found reams of the pink paper used to print the Communist pamphlet found at the bombing of Palmer's home. This in turn led to Roberto Elia and Andrea Salcedo, who admitted to being part of the Lynn, Massachusetts, group that had planned the bombing. The bomber who had blown himself up was believed to have been Carlo Valdinoci. Elia and Salcedo were arrested, but other members of the group had fled to Italy. The two were kept in custody on the fourteenth floor of a building in New York. During the night, while his guards and companions were asleep, Salcedo managed to open a window and jump to his death, so he could never reveal the truth.

Things began to go against Palmer. He was sued by Salcedo's widow, who claimed that harassment had led to the suicide, and by the widow of another man arrested who had died of untreated tuberculosis and pneumonia while in custody. The acting secretary of labor released 130 of those scheduled for deportation, on the grounds that they had been arrested without warrants.

J. Edgar Hoover and other Justice Department employees urged Congress to impeach Louis Post, the acting secretary of labor, but the effort backfired. At his impeachment hearing, Post read aloud from some of the warrants to show that they were so vague as to be worthless. He charged that Palmer had lied about the anarchists and other protesters being armed, that only three pistols had been confiscated from those arrested. He accused Palmer of acting on his own without proper authorization from the president. Unfortunately, President Wilson had had a stroke and could not testify as to what he had said to Palmer and when. Palmer received death threats, and there were calls for his resignation.

Just when events were looking the worst for Palmer, a series of wildcat railroad strikes upset the country. Palmer went to the White House and persuaded the president's doctors to arrange a Cabinet meeting. The president was propped up while Palmer declared before the group that these strikes were the work of socialist or Communist agitators. Afterward he told the press that he had the president's authority to break the strikes with force, and the walkouts dissolved. No one came forward to say that the president was not in a condition to make any decisions. The acting secretary of labor declared that the strikes were not politically motivated.

Palmer predicted that a general Communist uprising would take place on May 1, 1920, the international Labor Day. Police departments across America were put on alert, but as the day came and went, no insurrection occurred. Palmer and the Justice Department were further discredited. Then Congress said that he might have to appear before the Rules Committee to refute Louis Post's accusations. Palmer was able to prove that many weapons had been seized from protesters, but Congress decided not to impeach Post, so Palmer again lost face.

Palmer still thought that he might win the Democratic nomination for president, and at the opening of the convention, he was third in the most committed delegates. But his nickname, "The Fighting Quaker," was ridiculed as the "Fighting Quacker" and "The Quaking Fighter." Wilson refused to endorse either Palmer or the president's son-in-law, William McAdoo, indicating that he himself wanted a third term. Palmer had no support from labor unions because he had broken up strikes and arrested union members, and he lost out on the thirty-ninth ballot to Governor James Cox of Ohio.

Even though a bomb on Wall Street on September 16 killed twenty-nine people and may well have been the work of anarchists, Palmer's charges were ignored, and the crime was never solved. Had it happened a year earlier, the attack would have been part of his "Red Raid" hysteria, but his lawless methods of tamping down dissent had discredited his crusade.

Twenty admitted Communists were convicted and sentenced to prison, including the wealthy William Bross Lloyd, who had actually felt neglected when Palmer did not arrest him in the first wave of raids. Lloyd wanted to make a public statement of his beliefs and had bragged to a reporter of being a Communist. Bolshevik leader Vladimir Lenin's representative in New York was deported, and many anarchists fled. The Labor Department eventually agreed with Palmer's charges for 820 of those being held, and they were deported in 1921. Palmer's main legacy was a sharp drop in Communist Party membership, from sixty thousand to less than ten thousand.

And of course he launched the Red-hunting career of J. Edgar Hoover.

Warren Harding won election in 1920 by a landslide, a further repudiation of Wilson and his representative, Mitchell Palmer.

At the end of Wilson's term, Palmer returned to private law practice. He remained active in the Democratic Party and helped write the platform for Franklin Roosevelt's winning presidential campaign in 1932. Palmer died on May 11, 1936, believing to the last that he had saved America from a possible overthrow by Communists and anarchists.

SOURCES

I began my research with the chapter "A. Mitchell Palmer: Seeing Red," in Michael Farquhar's *A Treasury of Great American Scandals* (New York: Penguin Books, 2003) and *The Big Bad Book of Democrats* by Lawrance Binda (Washington, D.C: Pazzo Press, 2005). I also read *Perilous Times: Free Speech in Wartime from the Sedition Act of 1798 to the War on Terrorism* by Geoffrey R. Stone (New York: W.W. Norton, 2004); *From the Palmer Raids to the Patriot Act* by Christopher M. Finan (Boston: Beacon Press, 2007); Curt Gentry's *J. Edgar Hoover—The Man and the Secrets* (New York: W.W. Norton, 1991); and especially interesting, Kenneth D. Ackerman's *Young J. Edgar: Hoover, the Red Scare and the Assault on Civil Liberties* (New York: Carroll & Graf Publishers, 2007).

For the way Palmer's raids and the bombings were perceived at the time, I consulted various newspapers: *The Chester Times* of Chester, Pennsylvania, November 9, 1919, page 1, "Suppress Russian Workers Union Aim of Red Raids." *Lowell Sun,* Lowell Massachusetts, November 10, 1919, page 1, "Nationwide Roundup." *The Marion Daily Star*, Marion, Ohio, June 3, 1919, page 1, "Reds Bomb Homes and Start Reign of Terror." *The Steubenville Weekly Herald,* Steubenville, Ohio, November 13, 1919, page 3, "Raids on Alleged Plotters Against the Government," and page 10, "Nets Are Laid to Nab Reds." *Tyrone Daily Herald*, Tyrone, Pennsylvania, June 4, 1919, page 1, "Bombs Planted in Many Cities."

I also found information on the Federal Bureau of Investigation's Web site, www.fbi.gov/page2/dec07/palmerraids122807.html, accessed March 2, 2010.

CHAPTER FOURTEEN

Warren G. Harding:
The "He-Harlot"

Warren Harding was a better president than he has been given credit for, but he was a jerk as a husband. His wife, Florence Kling Harding, was the most popular first lady since Dolley Madison and was largely responsible for his successful political career. He praised her in public utterances and acknowledged the debt he owed her, but throughout their marriage he cheated on her with a series of women, including her best friend. If Harding had been a woman, one critic said, he'd have been called a harlot.

The Hardings' marriage was the first of several presidential marriages in which the press covered up a weak-willed husband's sexual indiscretions.

Warren was a handsome man, amiable and well liked, especially by women. Even his father said of him, "Warren, it's a good thing you aren't a woman, or you'd be continually in the family way. You can't say no."

Florence was the eldest child of Amos and Louisa Kling. Amos, the richest man in Marion, Ohio, taught Florence business and accounting, had her help out in his hardware store, and saw to it that she received a good education. She had musical talent and attended a conservatory of music in Cincinnati. But she resented parental control, and at nineteen she became pregnant and lived as the common-law wife of her baby's father, Henry deWolfe. When Henry abandoned her and baby Marshall, Florence was destitute. She supported herself and her child by giving piano lessons. Her father agreed to support her if she would relinquish custody of the child to him. She did.

Enter Warren Harding.

Florence Harding says goodbye to the White House staff as she and President Harding leave on a trip. Warren had gone on many trips without her, rendezvousing with other women.
LIBRARY OF CONGRESS

Both of Warren's parents were doctors, and he was sent to Ohio Central College at age fourteen with the idea that he too might become a doctor. Warren was intelligent but seldom studied. He worked his way through college with a series of jobs, and he and a friend established a college newspaper.

After his graduation, his father financed Warren's purchase of the *Marion Daily Star*, a struggling newspaper and one of three in the town. Warren was only nineteen. In 1884 he attended the Republican National Convention, using the free railroad pass that newspapermen were given, even though he was not old enough to vote. Journalism and politics captured his time and attention from then on.

As editor and owner of the newspaper, Warren campaigned for streetlights, streetcars, and an orchestra for Marion, and wrote an editorial against the "rent-gouging landlord" Amos Kling, soon to be his father-in-law. By 1890 Harding had expanded the newspaper to eight pages and added a supplement, *Star Weekly*, which was pro-Republican.

Florence was teaching piano lessons to Warren's sister Charity when she met the handsome newspaper editor. She fell in love and made opportunities to be with him, even interrupting his chats with other women. She stated later that she found him "interesting" and could see that he had a bright future. Despite his later reputation as a lightweight nonintellectual, Harding was intelligent and well read and could converse on a variety of subjects. Perhaps he was attracted to Florence because she took him seriously, indicating that he could become a great man. Or perhaps he was intrigued by the experienced, practical Florence, who was five years older than he.

The two were married at their new home on July 8, 1891. Florence's father had prevented their having the wedding at the Methodist church, but he couldn't keep the three hundred guests from attending. One of them was Florence's mother, who defied her husband to see her daughter married. Florence was interested in astrology, and insisted that the wedding must begin promptly at 8:00 p.m. and end by 8:30. The minister rushed through the ceremony, ending just in the nick of time to avoid possible doom. Florence showed her independence by refusing to wear a wedding ring.

After the newlyweds returned from their honeymoon, Florence gave up teaching piano and turned her attention to the finances of the newspaper. She soon got the accounts in order, making the newspaper more profitable.

Throughout his life Warren was subject to poor health, despite his robust appearance. He smoked, chewed tobacco, drank, took little exercise, and had frequent bouts of stomach pain. Eighteen months after their marriage, he had a "nervous breakdown," the second in four years, and spent time at the Kellogg Sanitarium in

Battle Creek, Michigan. While he was there, the *Star*'s business manager quit, and Florence took over. She organized the newspaper delivery boys, sometimes punishing them for bad behavior. Many went on to successful careers and were her lifelong friends and supporters.

Meanwhile, perhaps resenting Florence's expectations of him or merely taking advantage of an easy opportunity, Warren had a brief fling with a neighbor, Susie Hodder, a childhood friend of Florence's. In 1895, in Nebraska, Susie gave birth to Warren's daughter, named Marion in honor of her hometown. Warren supported the child, and Florence knew of the affair and the child, but hid her anger and shame, confiding only to her diary.

Warren began attending Republican events, where his good looks and marvelous speaking voice attracted attention. In Marion, their home was the social gathering place.

In 1899, Warren won his first election, to the Ohio state legislature, and in Columbus he and Florence met Harry Daugherty, attorney and lobbyist, who was to be a part of their lives from then onward. He claimed to have been the first to declare what a "great-looking president" Harding would make.

After two terms in the Ohio Senate, Harding was elected lieutenant governor. He and Florence traveled the Chautauqua circuit, where he made well-received speeches. They were invited to Texas and New York, and Ohio Congressman Nicholas Longworth invited them to Washington. They took a Hawaiian cruise and spent time in Florida at the Kling winter home. Florence's father had finally accepted Warren, and Warren got along well with Florence's son, Marshall.

Warren and Florence often socialized with their neighbors, the Phillipses. Jim Phillips owned a large department store in Marion. His wife, Carrie, buxom and beautiful, was Florence's friend and confidante, though she was fifteen years younger.

Life was going well for the Hardings—for a while.

The Phillipses' child died, and the Hardings consoled them. Then Florence was struck down with nephritis, due to a small "floating" kidney blocking the other. She was taken to Columbus for surgery, during which the kidney was tacked into place. While she was recuperating, Jim Phillips suffered depression and a "nervous breakdown." Warren arranged for him to go to the sanitarium in Battle Creek, promising to look after Carrie in his absence. He did, indeed. While their two spouses were ill, Warren and Carrie began an affair that lasted for the next fifteen years.

After their spouses returned to Marion, Warren and Carrie would meet in her garden at night, with Warren telling Florence that he needed to take a walk after dinner. He wrote passionate letters to Carrie, knowing that she would be home to receive them before Jim returned from the store. Carrie sent him letters to the newspaper office, with a fake return address. Warren arranged a trip to Europe for the two couples and continued his affair on the voyage across the Atlantic. At night while Florence slept in their cabin, Warren met Carrie on the dark deck outside for sex.

By this time, the Hardings had reorganized the newspaper into the Harding Publishing Company, and it was bringing in enough money for Warren to buy a touring car and Florence to have live-in household help. What she lacked was a husband's love and attention. Following her return from the hospital, he had taken her on a trip to Jamaica, but during the following summer he often went out of town "on business" and met Carrie at hotels across the state.

The two couples took another trip to Europe and Egypt together, and in 1911, the four vacationed together in Bermuda.

Carrie urged Warren to divorce Florence. She would then divorce Jim, and the two lovers could marry. Warren, realizing that he needed Florence financially and politically, stalled Carrie. She first attempted to make Warren jealous by sending him letters from one of her earlier lovers and then brought the affair out in the open by writing him a passionate letter addressed to him at home. Florence opened it and was outraged and devastated. She'd been betrayed by her husband and her best friend, the two people she was closest to.

Florence considered divorce, but her options were limited. She would have adequate money from the publishing company and could go back to her father's house or get an apartment, but she would be an object of scorn and pity in Marion.

Warren didn't want a divorce either. He wanted to keep the situation as it was with both women, and that's what happened.

Warren ran unsuccessfully for the Ohio governorship and for a time concentrated on running the newspaper and campaigning for other Republicans.

Carrie moved to Germany. Soon she was sending Warren descriptions of her German lovers. Twice she sailed to New York for a weekend tryst with Warren. Each time he told Florence he was going elsewhere.

In 1912 Warren was asked to make the nominating speech for William H. Taft, who was running for reelection as president. It made no difference. The enmity between Taft and Teddy Roosevelt split the Republican Party, and Democrat Woodrow Wilson was elected.

In 1913, Florence and Warren made another trip to Europe, and she wrote back her impressions as regular columns for the *Star*. Warren made no effort to contact Carrie in Europe.

Back home, Florence faced other crises. Her son, Marshall, married and living in Arizona, was in poor health and in debt. Her father died in October of that year, and Florence herself was ill again and spent time in a nearby clinic run by Dr. Charles Sawyer. "Doc," as the Hardings called him, was to play a prominent role from then on in the Hardings' lives—and deaths.

Meanwhile, another sticky situation was brewing, though neither Florence nor Warren recognized it as such at the time. A neighbor and friend, Sam Britton, died, and Warren was able to get a teaching job for his widow. The Brittons' daughter, Nan, had a crush on Warren, declaring it openly to her schoolmates. She was as persistent as Florence had been in pursuing Warren, with results that forever damaged his reputation.

Warren urged Carrie to come home as he sensed the impending war in Europe. Eventually she returned, just before World War

I began. Warren and Carrie resumed their affair, but politics was his real mistress.

In 1914 Senator Theodore Burton of Ohio decided to retire, and Florence urged Warren to run for the seat. Florence had regained her health and campaigned vigorously. Warren had mixed feelings. If Florence had died, he would be free to marry Carrie, who did not want him in politics. But politics called. He was elected U.S. senator.

Warren and Florence moved to Washington and lived for a while in the Willard Hotel until Florence found the right house. She'd inherited a small fortune from her father and spent it making the Harding home attractive. Jess Smith, a colleague of Harry Daugherty's, was especially good at choosing fabrics and designs, and Florence shopped in New York with his assistance and with Evalyn Walsh McLean, mining heiress and Washington hostess. Florence also took Warren to a good tailor and had him outfitted in the way she thought a senator should dress.

In the Senate, Warren had an affair with one of his secretaries, Grace Cross, and also began carousing with other senators and Washington figures, including Ned McLean, Evalyn's husband and owner of the *Washington Post*. The men drank while playing poker well into the night. Call girls accompanied them.

Nan Britton graduated from high school and went to New York to study secretarial work. She wrote to Harding asking for his help in finding her a job. He responded by letter and arranged to meet her in New York. They stayed at hotels under assumed names and began an affair. Nan was twenty, Warren fifty. She began to make trips to Washington and claimed that she conceived his child when they had sex in his Senate office. Warren gave her money and urged her to have an abortion, as did her sister, but Nan refused. She moved to Chicago and lived with her sister, who adopted the child, Elizabeth Ann.

The war in Europe drew America in, with great loss of life and a big debt. A disastrous flu epidemic followed. By the time of the 1920 election, Americans were tired of problems and opposed to entering the League of Nations, which they felt would only involve America in more European problems.

Although Harding had had an undistinguished senatorial career, he was asked to be the keynote speaker at the 1916 Republican Convention, and in 1920 was a contender for the presidential nomination, along with nine others. Florence's astrologer had predicted that Warren would be nominated after noon on the final day of the convention—which was also the last day that he could file for reelection to the Senate. Florence and Harry Daugherty urged him to hold out for the nomination, and gradually enough votes were swayed so that he was nominated as the astrologer had predicted. When the convention leaders asked him if there was any reason why he could not accept the nomination, Harding stepped outside for a moment, considered Nan and his other women, and said no. He had met with Nan secretly during the convention.

Nan was not the immediate problem; Carrie was. She demanded thousands of dollars not to make his letters to her public. Part of his campaign money went to pay her off with a lump sum, to send her and her husband on a yearlong trip around the world, and, if he were elected, to pay her a certain amount each year as long as he held the office of president. Grace Cross was also paid off.

Florence may have privately berated Warren for all his misdeeds that might cost him the election, but publicly she swung into action, campaigning as no political wife before her had done. She had a separate office built in the backyard of their Marion house, and here they spent the summer, receiving fans and the press. Over sixty thousand people called at the Hardings' office during the campaign, including movie stars and political celebrities. Newsreel cameras rolled. Florence willingly chatted with the press and posed for photos, always saying flattering things about her husband and downplaying her own role.

She consulted her favorite Washington astrologer, who predicted that Warren would win but that either he or Florence would die before the four-year term ended.

Warren won. He continued his nightly poker playing and drinking, and his only exercise was golf. He worked long hours at the presidency, learning what needed to be done. The job was stressful.

Florence was the first woman ever to vote for her husband for president, and as first lady, was the first to ride in an airplane. She took on causes that kept her in the public eye: animal rights, women's rights, and especially the treatment of wounded veterans. The appointment of Charlie Forbes, a smooth-talking colleague of the Hardings, to the Veterans Bureau, was to ruin her work.

Warren continued his affair with Nan, arranging with the Secret Service to bring her to his office by a secluded back door, but he never acknowledged Elizabeth Ann as his child and never saw her.

In the autumn of 1922, Florence came near death from another serious kidney ailment. She knew by this time that Forbes was stealing and selling supplies from the veterans' hospitals, which added to her stress. Her illness affected Warren, who realized how much he depended on her, but few noticed his deteriorating health. The president had shortness of breath and had to be propped up in bed at night to sleep.

In early 1923, the Hardings and the McLeans vacationed in Florida, where Warren had pneumonia and where an attempt was made on Florence's life. When she was making a speech, someone tossed her a bouquet of flowers. Fortunately, her Secret Service agent caught it. Had she sniffed the flowers, she would have inhaled acid. Was it from one of Warren's women? Or someone who blamed Florence's support of Forbes for the privation of veterans? The person who tossed the bouquet was not identified.

Back in Washington, Warren rewrote his will and made arrangements to sell the publishing company for $500,000, although he had talked of being a one-term president, after which he would return to Marion and the newspaper. Did he have a premonition of death?

Despite Warren's weakened condition, the Hardings went ahead with a summer trip to the Western states and Alaska. Florence and Warren had longed to see Alaska, and the trip had twice been postponed. The presidential train set out in early July, crossing the continent with frequent stops for speeches to adoring crowds. The Hardings transferred to a steamer for the trip up the coast. Despite Warren's shakiness and pallor, he made speeches and received the usual trophies and accolades. The scenery thrilled both Hardings, and Warren predicted a bright future for the territory.

As the presidential party made its way down the coast to San Francisco, various people noted the frailty of the president. At one point, many in the group had food poisoning, but Warren didn't "snap back" afterward as the others did.

As Warren grew sicker, Doc Sawyer, who had accompanied the group along with a younger doctor, Joel Boone, repeatedly gave Warren purgatives. Boone protested that this was the worst possible treatment, but Doc was jealous of his position as White House physician and would accept no advice from a younger man. He also refused to call in heart specialists or to transfer Warren to a hospital where his life might have been extended.

Warren Harding died on August 2, 1923, sometime after 7:00 p.m. at the Palace Hotel in San Francisco. There were conflicting reports of the exact time of death, of who had been at the president's bedside at the moment of death, and even of the cause of death. Doc insisted it was a stroke, and the other doctors present reluctantly signed the death certificate that indicated "cerebral hemorrhage" rather than "cardiac arrest."

Florence burned many of Warren's papers, but his secretary, George Christian, managed to save several boxes of them and transport them safely to Marion. Friends of Warren's raised money to build a monument to him in Marion, where he and Florence are buried.

Florence lived only another year, but long enough to see Warren accused of huge corruption and herself accused of killing him.

All evidence, however, indicates that Harding died of congestive heart failure. The final blow to his reputation came from Nan Britton. Harding had left her nothing in his will, and after a short time, his relatives ceased supporting her. She wrote a book, *The President's Daughter*, detailing their affair, and enemies of Harding made it a best seller. Contemporaries and historians think much of it was fabricated.

As president, Warren Harding signed the peace treaty with Germany and Austria ending World War I, established the Veterans Bureau, signed a treaty indemnifying Colombia for the loss of Panama, presided at the Washington Naval Conference, reduced the national debt, established the Bureau of the Budget, and pardoned Eugene V. Debs, who had been wrongly imprisoned for treason by Woodrow Wilson. Harding was the first sitting senator to be elected president and the first to hold a press conference. He wanted to lower taxes, end lynching, and give women more rights, but his death ended those plans, and he is remembered mainly for scandals.

Most of the letters Warren wrote to Carrie Phillips are sealed by court order until 2023, but the few that have leaked out give ample evidence of Warren as a philanderer, a "he-harlot."

SOURCES

I read the classic Harding biographies: *The Shadow of Blooming Grove: Warren G. Harding in His Times* by Francis Russell (New York: McGraw-Hill, 1968) and Robert K. Murray's extensive biography, *The Harding Era*, published the following year by the University of Minnesota Press. I also read *Warren G. Harding*, one in the American Presidents series, by John W. Dean and Arthur M. Schlesinger (New York: Henry Holt, 2004) and *Dead Last: The Public Memory of Warren G. Harding's Scandalous Legacy* by Phillip Payne, published in 2009 by the Ohio University Press at Athens, Ohio. Harding is prominently featured in *The Teapot Dome Scandal* by Laton McCartney (New York: Random House, 2008). My favorite book on the Hardings was *Florence Harding: The First*

Lady, the Jazz Age and the Death of America's Most Scandalous President by Carl Sferrazza Anthony (New York: William Morrow, 1998). This gave me a real appreciation of America's first modern first lady, a working woman, campaigner, supporter of causes—and loyal wife, though Warren Harding didn't deserve her.

CHAPTER FIFTEEN

A Pair of Federal Thieves:
Fall and Forbes

When Warren G. Harding first took his seat in the U.S. Senate, Senator Albert B. Fall welcomed him to the "gentlemen's club." It was to be a disastrous friendship for both men, ending with a forever-tarnished reputation for Harding and jail for Fall.

Shortly before taking office, Senator-elect Harding and his wife, Florence, met charming Charlie Forbes during a trip to Hawaii. Forbes betrayed the Hardings so badly that when Warren discovered the betrayal, he tried to choke Forbes.

Both Fall and Forbes enriched themselves by disposing of government property, made possible by their friendship with the Hardings and their position in Warren Harding's administration.

Fall and Forbes were different in their personalities, backgrounds, and type of crime, but alike in their ruthless disregard for the president and the American people.

On the Hawaii trip in 1914, Harding, noted for his melodious speaking voice, was speaker at a number of official functions, and Forbes probably saw him as a "comer."

Charlie Forbes stole not only from the taxpayers, but from helpless, wounded veterans.
LIBRARY OF CONGRESS

Albert Fall was the "fall guy," receiving stiffer punishment than his cocriminals in the Teapot Dome Scandal.

Forbes, an amiable, personable man, was what would later be called "slick" or "Teflon." He had managed to be put in charge of building the Pearl Harbor Naval Base by Democratic president Woodrow Wilson, even though Forbes considered himself a Republican. Moreover, he had deserted from the U.S. Army fifteen years earlier, was apprehended by the army after four years AWOL, and was reinstated without a court-martial. His record showed an honorable discharge in 1907.

If Harding knew all this, he didn't care. He enjoyed playing poker with Forbes, and Florence Harding liked Forbes's wife, Kate. In the years between their Hawaii meeting and the time Harding became president, Forbes served with distinction in World War I, achieving the rank of lieutenant colonel. He settled afterward in Washington State, where he saw to it that the votes of that state went to Harding in the 1920 presidential election. For his party loyalty, Harding considered him briefly as governor of the Philippines and also offered him the governorship of Alaska, but Forbes was not interested in either post.

Harding appointed him head of the Bureau of War Risk Insurance. This agency looked after veterans who were suffering from mental illness, tuberculosis, and other ills, and Florence Harding thought their friend Charlie would do a good job for the veterans. One of her favorite projects was the care of wounded veterans. She spent a great deal of time visiting military hospitals, seeing that the wounded received good medical care, supplies, and personal attention.

When President Harding decided to form the Veterans Bureau, combining the Bureau of War Risk Insurance with the Federal Hospitalization Bureau, he put Forbes in charge of the new organization. Forbes persuaded the president to add the Quartermaster General Department and the architectural group responsible for building military hospitals to the Veterans Bureau. Harding did, by executive order, without congressional action.

With such opportunities for graft, Forbes soon became wealthy. He put his friends on the payroll with nonexistent jobs, demanded kickbacks from contractors who built hospitals, and overvalued land on which hospitals were to be built, with a portion of the purchase price going to him. Worst of all, he sold off medical supplies and other items belonging to the veterans and pocketed the proceeds. He persuaded the Bureau of the Budget to allow him to sell the "surplus" items, claiming they were deteriorated and worthless. He sold drugs and alcohol straight to illegal dealers. Tools and thousands of trucks were sold at a fraction of their value to a Boston firm, Thompson & Kelley. In return for the bargains, the firm "loaned" money to Forbes. Bandages, pajamas, sheets, and towels, many still in their original wrapping, were sold at less than a tenth of their cost. At the same time, Forbes was ordering new items at exorbitant prices. For example, he bought a hundred-year supply of floor wax for nearly a dollar a gallon, when it was for sale on the open market at four cents a gallon! Overpaying for military items did not begin or end with Forbes, but he carried it to extremes.

Rumors of the fixed sales began to spread, and Harding's physician reported the graft to him. The president sent for Forbes, who came with deliberately damaged goods and said he was selling them to save the storage cost, which he represented at twenty times more than it actually was. Then Harding's attorney general, Harry Daugherty, told the president that the stories were true. Harding refused to believe Daugherty until he investigated himself, making a trip to one of the warehouses. He sent for Forbes again, cursed him, and was seen by a visitor choking the cheating Forbes. Harding allowed Forbes to go to Europe and submit his resignation from there.

Forbes was later prosecuted for embezzlement and served two years in prison. It was estimated that he stole $250 million from the Veterans Bureau, a fantastic sum considering that the bureau's entire budget for those three years was $1.3 billion.

This was the first of the Harding administration scandals, but the only one that Harding knew about. He died before learning what Fall, his secretary of the interior had done with the government oil reserves known as the Teapot Dome.

Fall hadn't been Harding's first choice for interior secretary, and he only got the job because of an affair that ended in murder. Jake Hamon, an oil millionaire from Oklahoma, had been the intended secretary. He had borrowed money and spread it around in the right places so that votes went toward Harding. In return he'd planned that as secretary of the interior he could get control of the Teapot Dome oil and share it with friends and backers, including oil millionaire Harry Sinclair. There was a small problem: Jake was married to Florence Harding's cousin but was separated from her and living with his mistress, Clara. Florence demanded that he reconcile with his wife before coming to Washington. When Jake attempted to break off with Clara, she shot him. He died shortly thereafter.

Harding's next choice was Herbert Hoover, but Hoover preferred the top position at the Department of Commerce. Fall, Harding thought, might be right for secretary of state, since he was an international lawyer and had lived and worked in Mexico. Harding was persuaded that the hot-tempered Fall was unsuited for a diplomatic position and instead chose Charles Evans Hughes as secretary of state.

So Fall became secretary of the interior. He could scarcely have done worse for the country and for Harding's reputation if he had been the top diplomat.

Fall was born in Kentucky in 1861 and at an early age went to work in the cotton mills. By the time he was eighteen, he was supporting himself by teaching school as well as doing farm work. He had health problems and moved west, to the dry climate of the New Mexico Territory. He worked as a cowboy, driving herds to market, then as a camp cook, all the while educating himself in law. The coming of the railroads meant the end of the cattle drives, and thus the end of his job. Fall moved to Texas, worked as a bookkeeper, and married Emma Morgan. The couple moved to Mexico, where Albert was involved in mining. In 1885, the Falls moved to New Mexico.

There, he met Edward Doheny, a prospector. The friendship was to last a lifetime and be significant for both men.

Mining, however, was not profitable for Fall. He moved his growing family to Las Cruces, New Mexico, where he passed his bar exam and set up a law practice. In 1888 he ran for the legislature as a Democrat, but the Republicans controlled the territory and he lost to another Albert: Albert Fountain. Republicans were in charge of the sale of supplies to the Indian reservations as well as the appointment of public officials, including judges. In the following election, Fall won, and two years later Grover Cleveland, a Democrat, was elected president. In 1893 Fall was appointed judge of the circuit court, the youngest judge of his time, only thirty-two.

In 1896 his nemesis, Albert Fountain, and Fountain's young son disappeared while driving their wagon between Lincoln and Las Cruces. Neither body was ever found, though three men who had been involved in cattle rustling and threatening locals were tried for the Fountain murders. Albert Fall successfully defended them. The charges against one suspect were dropped, and the other two men were acquitted. The Fountain family believed that Fall had played a part in the murders.

Despite the rumors, Fall was elected president of the New Mexico Bar Association and served a one-year term as U.S. attorney of New Mexico. After the territory became a state, the legislature selected Fall to be one of New Mexico's first two U.S. senators. Republicans objected because Fall had only recently become a Republican and thus did not deserve the position, but he went to Washington in 1912. The Democrats didn't like him either, claiming he had abandoned the party. However, he was reelected in 1918, though some felt it was because of sympathy for his family. His son and one of his three daughters had died of influenza shortly before the election.

Fall now considered himself a Republican, and when the affable Republican Warren Harding was elected to the Senate from Ohio, Fall was quick to make his acquaintance.

On the morning of his presidential inauguration, Harding dropped by the Senate chamber, presented his list of Cabinet appointees, and asked that they all be confirmed. The entire slate was approved within minutes, with no discussion, so no history or misdeeds of any candidates were brought up.

Charlie Forbes's crimes were straightforward and easy to detect. Fall's crime was more complex and resulted in legal wrangling that went on for nearly a decade. Some apologists claim that Fall committed no crime but instead acted for patriotic reasons that had to remain secret.

It's hard to believe that Fall, when accused of a crime, would not have brought out any evidence to exonerate himself, especially before his former colleagues, the U.S. Senate. After all, he was a former trial lawyer. Testimony could even have been taken in the secrecy of closed chambers. Juries found him guilty not once, but three times, of oil deals involving the Teapot Dome reserve and other leases.

The Teapot Dome got its name from a strangely shaped rock formation atop the oil field in Wyoming. As America's ships turned from burning coal to oil, then-President William H. Taft set aside over nine thousand acres of known oil-rich land in the Teapot Dome area. Additional oil fields, including nearby Salt Creek in Wyoming and Elk Hills and Buena Vista in California, were also reserved for the use of the U.S. Navy. The U.S. government was to own these in perpetuity and could from time to time, as needed, allow companies to drill in the reserves. In return, the government would receive as payment a percentage of the oil removed, not in cash but in oil to be stored in federally owned tanks, or certificates good for oil or construction projects.

Soon after his appointment as secretary of the interior, Fall asked the secretary of the navy to turn over control of the oil reserves to the Department of the Interior. After all, he argued, much of the property was far in the interior of the country, not convenient to naval facilities. President Harding signed the transfer. With a few strokes of his pen, Harding transferred one-eighth of all the oil lands in the continental United States into the hands of a man he thought to be honest, but Fall was also a man in debt and a man who thought all the resources of the West should be exploited. His views were known, but ignored by Harding. Fall had earlier said that he thought the Department of the Interior should control only the national parks. All other land should be in private hands.

Leaders of the conservation movement thought the opposite. People such as former President Theodore Roosevelt, Gifford Pinchot, and Robert La Follette believed that America's riches should be saved for the benefit of future generations. They were appalled by the attitude of early pioneers, who had slaughtered Indians and buffalo alike, stripped the land of forests, and plundered the underground minerals. The exploiters were now in charge.

Reports arrived on the president's desk from mining engineers protesting that wells drilled by private companies just outside the reserve were draining the pool of oil underground. Thus, unless the government took steps to allow drilling, its oil lands might become drained and useless. Fall, of course, knew just the men who could best handle the large-scale drilling.

Without any competitive bidding, he awarded a lease for the entire 9,481-acre Teapot Dome oil field for twenty years to Harry Sinclair. Sinclair formed the aptly named Mammoth Oil Company, the stock of which he totally owned, to handle the oil from Teapot Dome. Under the terms of an earlier act, money from the oil reserves was to go to the Treasury Department, with the navy being allotted only half a million dollars. Sinclair agreed instead to build steel oil storage tanks at Pearl Harbor and a pipeline from Teapot Dome to join with another pipeline at Chicago.

Drilling rights for the Elk Hills reserve went to Ed Doheny, Fall's friend and prospecting partner from years earlier, now referred to as the "Rockefeller of the West." Doheny's company, Pan American Petroleum and Transport Company, was to build additional storage tanks, fill them with oil, build a refinery in California, and build a pipeline from Elk Hills to the refinery. For this he was granted the rights to thirty thousand acres of proven oil land for fifteen years.

Soon the impoverished Albert Fall began to prosper.

He owned a huge spread near Tularosa, New Mexico. With combined ownership and leases, Fall controlled three-quarters of a million acres of grazing land, but his property was dilapidated and he hadn't paid taxes on it in eight years. His mining property in Mexico had been seized by the Mexican government in 1910, and he had not been compensated. He wanted the U.S. government to assume a protectorate over Mexico and look out for the interests of American citizens there. Fall was broke.

Soon after the oil leases changed hands, Fall was given $100,000 in cash as a "loan" from Doheny, delivered to his hotel in Washington, D.C. Fall paid his taxes and bought an adjoining ranch that controlled the headwaters of the streams that flowed through his property. Over the Christmas holiday in 1921, Sinclair and friends visited the ranch and soon sent Fall livestock as gifts: six heifers, a bull, two boars, four sows, and a thoroughbred horse. There was more money too, eventually $400,000 in all, in cash and Liberty bonds. Fall refurbished and landscaped the ranch house, relaid and paved the roads on his property, installed a hydroelectric plant and a new irrigation system, and bought still more land.

Sinclair benefited immediately, even before drilling began. The stock in his oil company doubled within a few weeks as word of the lease leaked out. He made millions on the stock appreciation alone.

Envious neighbors in New Mexico noticed Fall's sudden prosperity, and companies and private individuals who thought they had drilling rights in Wyoming and California protested. The Marines were sent to Wyoming to remove the errant drillers; the maneuver ended peacefully.

The conservationists caught on and protested. A congressional investigation into the oil leases began in the autumn of 1923, shortly after the death of President Harding. Senator Thomas J. Walsh of Montana was in charge, assisted by Burton Wheeler, the junior senator from Montana. The two worked doggedly on the case, tracing the bonds and cash.

Fall panicked. He tried to get a friend in Chicago to say that he had loaned Fall the money, but the friend refused. Fall and his wife went to New York and then to Florida, "for his health." He next tried to get Ned McLean, who owned the *Washington Post*, to say that he had made the loan. Walsh tried to subpoena McLean, who was "too sick" to return to Washington. Walsh went to Florida, where McLean (faced with a perjury charge) admitted that he had not made the loan and indeed didn't have that much money to spare. The Falls moved on to New Orleans, where Fall continued to claim poor health. Sinclair, meanwhile, had fled to Europe, and so was unavailable for testimony.

Eventually Doheny confessed that he had given Fall the money—but it wasn't a bribe, he said. It was a mortgage on the ranch. He was acquitted of bribery. Sinclair returned, testified that he had bought a third interest in the ranch, and was acquitted of bribery. He was jailed, however, for contempt of court and jury tampering after he sent thugs to threaten some of the jurors and offered a bribe to others. He served three months in jail.

Fall was found guilty of accepting a bribe, though neither of the two who had given him money was found guilty of offering one. Still in poor health, he was brought in an ambulance to begin serving his one-year jail term. His doctor testified that Fall was "at death's door." He was fined $100,000, which was still unpaid when he died—twelve years later. Doheny, who had presented a promissory note with the signature torn off as evidence of the "loan," later foreclosed on the Fall ranch.

The leases on the oil reserves were canceled, and the government recouped millions of dollars in benefit. The oil reserves proved extremely valuable during World War II.

Fall paid a heavy price for what was a poor return. Others profited far more. Forbes made millions by crime, and several others connected to the Harding administration "made out like bandits." Attorney General Harry Daugherty and his friend Jess Smith sold illegal liquor that had been seized by the government and sold permits for dealers to buy liquor during Prohibition—for medicinal purposes, they stated. William Burns, in charge of the Bureau of Investigation (later the FBI) ran that agency so poorly it was referred to as the Bureau of Easy Virtue. He issued pardons, tipped off people who might be raided, and continued to run his detective agency on the side. His friend and hanger-on, Gaston Means, sold illusions. He pretended to have influence with high-ranking government officials and took money to "fix" things—indictments, prosecutions, etc.—as well as preyed on gullible widows. He bragged that he had gotten away with every possible crime, including murder. He served no jail time.

Albert Fall was the "fall guy," and Teapot Dome has come to be the symbol of government corruption.

Sources

The Teapot Dome Scandal by Laton McCartney (New York: Random House, 2008) gave the most complete coverage of the affair. In his self-published book *The Politics of Scandal: A. B. Fall and the Teapot Dome Scandal* (Albuquerque, N.M.: Creative Designs, 1988), Herman B. Weisner attempts to defend Fall, claiming that he was acting for patriotic, not selfish, motives. *American Trials of the 20th Century* (Detroit: Visible Ink Press, 1994) edited by Edward W. Knappman has a good description of the Teapot Dome trial. The various scandals of the Harding administration were also covered in Francis Russell's *The Shadow of Blooming Grove: Warren G. Harding in His Times* (New York: McGraw-Hill, 1968), in *Florence Harding: The First Lady, the Jazz Age and the Death of America's Most Scandalous President* by Carl Sferrazza Anthony (New York: William Morrow, 1998), and in Robert K. Murray's *The Harding Era* (Minneapolis: The University of Minnesota Press, 1969.)

J. Edgar Hoover ruled over the FBI like an evil emperor for nearly five decades.

CHAPTER SIXTEEN

J. Edgar Hoover:
Keeper of Secrets

J. Edgar Hoover turned the Bureau of Investigation—in the early 1920s called the "Bureau of Easy Virtue"—into an effective, respected organization. But in so doing, he built an empire, with himself as emperor, powerful, secretive, and vindictive. He kept extensive files on enemies and friends alike, and used these as political blackmail. He controlled all publicity about the Federal Bureau of Investigation, as it was later named, shielding himself and the bureau from criticism, and he took credit for the work others did. He was admired, hated, and feared. No one dared fire him, so he remained the bureau's director as long as he lived.

John Edgar Hoover was a lifelong resident of Washington, D.C., born there in 1895, the youngest of four children. He had a stutter, which he overcame by speaking very fast, especially when he was debating in high school. This earned him the nickname "Speed," although some say he acquired the nickname because of the speed with which he delivered groceries for a local market to earn pocket money.

After college, he attended George Washington University Law School, paying his way by working at the Library of Congress. Here he learned indexing and cross-referencing, which he would later famously put to use at the FBI. He realized that by using the library's codes he could locate any item in the millions of items housed there. Could such codes also be used to locate people? Or, by changing a code, would it be possible to hide a person or an item from other searchers?

He passed the bar exam about the time World War I began. With the help of a relative, he got a draft-exempt job at the Justice Department. He might have enlisted, but he had to support his family. His father had lost his government job following a nervous breakdown, and despite forty-two years of work for the government, had no pension. Edgar's siblings had married and moved into homes of their own, leaving him to look after his parents.

Edgar was assigned to the Alien Enemy Bureau, an agency that handled legal questions pertaining to the millions of Germans residing in America, most of them recent immigrants. Edgar impressed his colleagues with his hard work and obvious dedication to the job. He dressed better than most of the other lawyers, always wearing a neatly pressed dark suit and a clean white shirt. He struck his bosses as someone who would "go places."

Edgar never married, though he was involved with several women. In 1918 he was dating a woman named Alice, the daughter of a Washington attorney. Edgar and Alice were invited to a friend's engagement party, and Edgar decided that night would be a good time to announce their engagement as well. Alice stood him up and soon after married someone else. He was understandably crushed. Later, he was involved with Lela Rogers, the mother of actress Ginger Rogers. Lela broke off their relationship, saying Edgar was "married to the FBI" and she would always have held second place in his life. Although Edgar was regularly photographed at nightclubs with showgirls and actresses, he never again seriously considered marriage. He did have a long relationship with Dorothy Lamour, but she married someone else.

His social companion thereafter was not female, but male: Clyde Tolson, an FBI lawyer who, only three years after being hired, become Edgar's second in command. The two men dined together and traveled together, but had separate homes. Rumors abounded that the two were homosexual lovers, though Hoover publicly assailed homosexuality.

Edgar made himself useful to Attorney General Mitchell Palmer after World War I ended. The country was in turmoil. Thousands of workers went on strike, including even policemen, and anarchists spoke openly about overthrowing the American government. Citizens clamored for action, and Palmer obliged them. Edgar cooperated, using membership lists of Communist organizations. He listed each name on an index card, then cross-referenced them geographically, so that if trouble broke out in a certain area, the Justice Department would know whom to arrest. Palmer saw to it that Edgar was promoted and given raises.

He was ready with information that got agitators deported. Officially this was the job of the Labor Department. Edgar befriended the commissioner general of immigration in the Labor Department who wanted to deport Emma Goldman and others but lacked evidence for a solid case against them. Edgar secured the evidence and watched at the dock as the deportees embarked for Russia.

Edgar later claimed he did not know of the beatings and mistreatment that often went along with the arrests of Communists in 1919 and 1920 until afterward. Perhaps, but it's more likely he didn't want to know. Many of the charges against those arrested were dropped, and convictions were overturned. Felix Frankfurter, who later became a judge, defended some of the accused. Hoover began a file on Frankfurter and had him investigated.

During the Harding years, 1920–1923, the reputation of the Bureau of Investigation sank. Attorney General Harry Daugherty used the bureau as a dumping ground for political appointees who pulled down a paycheck but did no work. Some were even involved in criminal activities themselves, using the bureau as cover. Edgar bided his time.

After Harding's death, President Calvin Coolidge's attorney general, Harlan Stone, intended to "clean house" at the bureau. He had heard of the hard-working, talented organizer J. Edgar Hoover and offered Hoover the job of acting director. Hoover said, "I'll accept on one condition: that hiring and promotion will be on merit alone." Stone replied that he wouldn't want it any other way. Edgar decreed that all agents would be either lawyers or accountants. He wrote out regulations for their dress and behavior, and procedures for how cases were to be handled. Within three years, Edgar went from acting director to director, a job he was to hold for life.

Prohibition led to smuggling and gangland murders. One infamous criminal of the era was John Dillinger. After an aborted attempt to capture him, during which federal agents and innocent bystanders were killed, the bureau enlisted the cooperation of Anna Sage, a Romanian immigrant who was a madam in Chicago. With her help, Melvin Purvis and other FBI agents shot and killed Dillinger, who was called Public Enemy Number One. Edgar called a press conference and publicly praised Purvis. Sage did not get the promised visa for her cooperation and was deported.

Over the next months, the FBI, often with Purvis leading the attack, took down Pretty Boy Floyd, Machine Gun Kelly and "Ma" Barker and her son. Purvis was a hero, and Edgar was jealous. He saw to it that Purvis was not put in charge of any further high-profile cases, and Purvis soon resigned. He had a series of jobs and later committed suicide.

Edgar wanted publicity for the bureau and himself. He cultivated the friendship of columnists Walter Winchell and Drew Pearson and leaked carefully worded rumors to the gossip columnists, who wrote favorable items about Edgar and the bureau. Soon Edgar was known nationwide, and little boys wanted to grow up to be FBI agents, called "G-men." When one reporter asked him if he had ever personally made an arrest, Edgar had to admit that he had not. However, he soon remedied that. Agents arranged for him to arrive on the scene and make an arrest that had been set up. It was photographed and appeared in newspapers, giving Edgar more publicity.

Edgar knew how and whom to flatter. He wrote incoming President Franklin Roosevelt a welcoming note, met with him at the White House, and indicated that he was at FDR's service. Because he had been appointed director by a Republican administration, Edgar had reason to fear that the Democratic president might replace him. However, FDR and Edgar recognized the value of each other and worked together. FDR gave Edgar permission to use wiretaps to gather information, something that had been forbidden to him earlier. In return, Edgar sent FDR regular bits of useful information.

Edgar and the president's wife, Eleanor, disliked each other intensely. The animosity began when Edgar investigated two of Mrs. Roosevelt's newly appointed aides. She sent him a sharp letter objecting to the investigation, and Edgar began surveillance of the first lady. Eleanor was naïve to think that her movements would go unnoticed. She was, after all, one of the most famous women in the world. Edgar knew when she was going to Chicago to meet with Joseph Lash, a friend twenty-five years her junior, and he had their adjoining rooms bugged. The results indicated an intimate, possibly sexual, relationship. The FBI also secured copies of loving letters Eleanor wrote to Lash and to Lorena Hickok, a lesbian newspaper writer.

By this time, Edgar had books and magazine articles published that were written by agents, under his byline. He cooperated with Hollywood studios in making films about the FBI—provided he could see and censor the material before it became public.

When World War II began, Roosevelt urged Hoover to cooperate with the British secret service, and Edgar imagined himself taking charge of all foreign security matters, though he had never left the United States except for a brief foray across the Mexican border one night.

To his dismay, however, one of his longtime rivals, William Donovan, was asked to form the Office of Strategic Services, or OSS. Edgar was in charge of security for much of the Western Hemisphere, and for a time also worked with the British. He was impressed that the British had managed to acquire the code-breaking ability of the Germans and the microdot method of passing information. He missed out on the information the microdots carried, however.

A German double agent, Dusko Popov, approached the British with microdot information indicating Japanese interest in Pearl Harbor. His German handlers sent him to New York, where he contacted Edgar. Edgar agreed to furnish him with enough information to keep the Germans from becoming suspicious, and in August 1941 presented a report on Popov's information to FDR. No action was taken on the report, and it was not forwarded to the army and navy commanders in Hawaii. Was Edgar at fault for not recognizing or emphasizing the urgency of the information, or was the president at fault? Had the report been acted on promptly, the American forces would have been alerted, and while the attack on Pearl Harbor would still have occurred, its effects would have been far less deadly.

After America entered the war, Edgar, on behalf of the FBI, took credit for breaking up a sabotage attempt by the Germans, when in fact the FBI had little to do with it. A group of Germans landed on Long Island in a submarine and came ashore with weapons and explosives. They were spotted by a lone man and gave him money to go away. One of the Germans, George Dasch, who had previously lived in America, had decided beforehand to turn in himself and his fellow spies, but he had a difficult time doing it. His first call to the FBI was treated as a crank call. By the time he convinced an agent of the truth, the other saboteurs had scattered. He gave the FBI names, and the others were rounded up and tried, with six of the eight convicted and executed. Dasch and one other, rather than being granted immunity, were given lengthy prison sentences.

Edgar bragged that the FBI had forestalled a terrorist plot.

FDR had used Edgar when it suited him, and he planned to fire the director as soon as the war was over, but the president died beforehand.

His successor, Harry Truman, was not impressed with Edgar. When Edgar sent the new president his usual flowery message of welcome and indicated that he was available whenever Truman needed his services, Truman replied tartly that if he needed Edgar, he could contact him through the attorney general. Edgar's relationship with Truman never recovered, but Truman did not fire him. He recognized that Edgar had entrenched himself and had the support of Congress. Edgar worked for the election of Thomas Dewey in 1948, thinking that he might be named attorney general or even a Supreme Court justice, but his hopes were dashed when Truman won.

Meanwhile, the director was growing rich. Wealthy friends gave him stock tips, and all kinds of favors came his way. The manager of Edgar's favorite restaurant in Washington never billed him for his nightly dinners there. Monthlong vacations to a posh California hotel owned by oil millionaire Clint Murchison were paid for by Murchison, not by Hoover and Tolson, and flights across the continent were at taxpayer expense, billed as "inspections" of various FBI offices. Murchison and Sid Richardson, another Texas oil baron, gave Edgar no-lose oil investments: If an oil well paid out, Edgar got a share of the profits; if it did not, he was not charged for any expenses. In return, Edgar saw to it that Congress voted to continue favorable tax treatment for oil and gas businesses, and he sometimes also facilitated leases of government-owned oil reserves for his friends.

He loved horse racing, and while he allowed himself to be photographed placing a bet at the $2 window, he actually placed huge bets, based on tips about "fixed" races from underworld figures. The setup was like his "investments" in oil wells: If he won, he collected; if his horse lost, he didn't have to pay up.

He was enriched too by book royalties, though he never wrote the books. *Masters of Deceit,* ostensibly by J. Edgar Hoover but actually written by FBI agents, became a best seller. Murchison, who owned a big share of the publishing company, decreed that the book would be published. Local FBI agents across America were told to publicize it and were given "reviews" to be used by friendly newspapers. The book sold a quarter million copies in hardback and over two million in paperback. Edgar and Clyde Tolson got half of the royalties, with the remainder divided among the bureau employees who had done the final writing. Edgar's contribution to the project was the use of his name. He also "wrote" articles for newspapers and magazines.

Edgar never paid for house repairs. In 1938, after his mother died, he bought a house and soon had it expanded, at bureau expense. FBI employees cut his grass and built a deck on the back of his house, and each year while he was on vacation, his house was refurbished and repainted at taxpayer expense. For his birthday, he let it be known which expensive gifts he wanted, and FBI employees took up a collection to buy the items. When he gave presents, they were always paid for by American taxpayers.

When "friendly" government officials requested damaging information from the FBI, Edgar sent a courier with an official letter indicating that he could not legally furnish that information. But the same courier carried the requested information on paper without the FBI letterhead and lacking a signature. This way, Edgar cooperated in underhanded deals but the paper trail indicated that he had refused an illegal request.

With the Nazis defeated at the end of World War II, Edgar needed a new enemy. The Russians obliged, taking control of Eastern Europe and parts of Asia. The Cold War had begun. Edgar's enemies from his youth, the Communists, were again his enemies.

This time there were no massive raids and arrests, but spies and suspected spies were routed out of various government agencies and innocent people became caught up in "commie-hunting." The House Un-American Activities Committee (HUAC) was formed, and many public figures were called to testify before it. There were some guilty parties. Elizabeth Bentley, a Vassar-educated, dedicated Communist, had worked for several government departments, including the War Board. She was a courier for eighty Communist sympathizers. She had sex with a man she met in a bar, and going through his pockets, discovered he worked for the U. S. Probation Department. Thinking the FBI had found her out, she turned herself in. She admitted to passing secrets to her Communist lover and implicated four other government employees, including Harry Dexter White, a former assistant secretary of the treasury. Whittaker Chambers, an editor of *Time*, accused Alger Hiss, a high-ranking State Department official, of passing secrets to the Russians. Judith Coplon, an FBI employee, was caught with a purse full of secret documents. The FBI had to show its own copies to prove her guilt. Edgar was humiliated at the leak.

Many Americans, led by a youthful idealized image of Communism, had joined Communist or Communist-sympathetic organizations in the 1930s. By the late 1940s most had changed their minds and regretted their youthful mistakes. But their indiscretions were in their records, and Edgar controlled the records.

The net was spread wide, bringing in authors, artists, producers, and Hollywood stars. One was actor Sterling Hayden, who was advised to go privately to Edgar and admit to having joined a Communist-backed youth organization. He did, and Edgar betrayed him, demanding names of other Communist sympathizers and hauling them before HUAC. The offenders, including Hayden, were blacklisted from appearing in films, their careers ruined. The FBI hounded actor Charlie Chaplin for years, but no charges ever stuck.

When the Central Intelligence Agency (CIA) was established, as a successor to the OSS, Hoover assumed that he would head it up. When he was passed over, he destroyed records that might have been useful to the CIA and forbade his agents from cooperating with the new agency.

Hoover was merciless with any employee he considered disloyal or critical or who dared question his orders. The offender would be transferred from post to post at short notice, until he resigned. Or he might be fired "with prejudice," the notation made on his record so that he could not secure another government job.

One group Edgar never went after was organized crime, often referred to as the Mafia or the mob. Edgar had drinks with crime bosses at New York's Stork Club, dined with them in Miami and Los Angeles, and accepted favors from them. They bragged, "Hoover is in our pocket." Some suspect he gave organized crime a pass because he had been photographed engaging in homosexual acts and wearing women's clothing. The mob had the photos. Publicly he attacked homosexuals, and dared not let proof get out of his own behavior.

By the election of 1960, Hoover had amassed enough embarrassing information on political candidates that he could influence the outcome. He knew Joseph Kennedy through crime bosses, knew that Kennedy had made his fortune through liquor smuggling during Prohibition, and knew that Kennedy was grooming his son John to be president. Hoover had noticed John from his days as a naval officer posted to Washington during World War II, when he carried on an affair with a pro-Nazi Swede, Inga Arvard. Hoover had tapes of their assignations as well as proof that John Kennedy was having an affair with his secretary in 1958, after he had married Jackie. John was also carrying on a liaison with Judith Campbell (later Exner), who was not only his sexual partner, but his courier with messages to mobster Sam Giancana.

Hoover favored Lyndon Johnson's candidacy, but when Kennedy won the Democratic nomination, Hoover's files on Kennedy convinced John and his brother Robert "Bobby" to offer Johnson the second spot.

The files also ensured that Hoover would keep his job. What he hadn't counted on was having Bobby Kennedy as his boss, the attorney general. Previous attorneys general had left the running of the FBI to Edgar, but not Bobby. Despite Edgar's protest that organized crime was not a big problem in America, Bobby set out to destroy the Mafia. Grudgingly Edgar had to cooperate. Giancana was especially angry: He and his colleagues had helped elect Kennedy and now they were being hounded. They vowed revenge.

The president went on flagrantly having affairs, protected by the press. Edgar discovered that Kennedy had had recent liaisons with several foreign prostitutes, one of whom was involved with the British Profumo scandal, involving a member of Parliament. The British prostitutes were also having sex with Russian officials, which could have been a serious security risk. Both Kennedy brothers had an affair with Marilyn Monroe. Edgar collected proof of it all, and used his leverage over Bobby to get authorization to wiretap Martin Luther King Jr. Edgar also guaranteed that he would not be forced to step down as director when he reached the age of seventy. But before that time, John was dead and Bobby had resigned.

Edgar managed to stall the investigation into President Kennedy's assassination, so that the truth may never be known.

He hung on to the job of director through Johnson's administration, but his world was coming to an end. Clyde Tolson had open heart surgery followed by several strokes. Edgar himself was weakening and was becoming the object of derisive jokes in Washington. President Nixon, whom Edgar had supported since Nixon's arrival in D.C. in 1947 as a newly elected congressman, wanted to get rid of him.

J. Edgar Hoover died on May 2, 1972. He was found on the floor beside his bed and was presumed to have died of natural causes, although there were rumors of poisoning. There was no autopsy. Before his body was removed, FBI agents searched his house, his office was locked, and many files were sealed.

He was eulogized, flags flew at half-staff, and his body lay in state in the nation's Capitol, an honor previously given to only twenty-one people. Of the thousands who filed past his bier, there must have been many who celebrated his demise.

SOURCES

Few dared to write anything critical of J. Edgar Hoover during his lifetime, but after his death the dirty linen has been aired. I read five of these tell-all books: *Young J. Edgar: Hoover, the Red Scare and the Assault on Civil Liberties* by Kenneth D. Ackerman (New York: Carroll & Graf Publishers, 2007); *The Director: An Oral History of J. Edgar Hoover* by Ovid Demaris (New York: Harper's Magazine Press, 1975); Curt Gentry's *J. Edgar Hoover—The Man and the Secrets* (New York: W.W. Norton, 1991); *The Bureau—The Secret History of the FBI* by Ronald Kessler (New York: St. Martin's Paperbacks, 2002); and *Official and Confidential—The Secret Life of J. Edgar Hoover,* by Anthony Summers (New York: Simon & Schuster, 1993).

Three bullies: Senator Joseph McCarthy and his henchmen (from left), David Schine and Roy Cohn.

CHAPTER SEVENTEEN

Joseph McCarthy:
Fearmonger

Senator Joseph McCarthy probably did more to lower the prestige of the American government, and destroyed more reputations, than anyone else up to that time. He fabricated charges against innocent people, faked his own records, and didn't even believe in the "cause" he was pursuing. He simply relished the attention of the press and the power he had over others. He jumped on the bandwagon of anti-Communist hysteria in America, bullying witnesses in Senate investigations until he was finally brought down.

For a while, he seemed the embodiment of the American success story.

At seventeen he was raising huge flocks of chickens on the family farm near Appleton, Wisconsin, but after a poultry disease wiped out his investment, he left the farm for a job clerking in a store. He soon rose to manager.

Deciding that he needed a profession, he persuaded the local high school principal to let him advance through courses at his own pace and completed the four-year curriculum in a single year. He enrolled in Marquette University, where he first studied engineering and then switched to law. He was president of his senior class, an early political victory.

McCarthy passed the bar in 1935, in the depths of the Depression. Setting up a law practice in Waupaca, Wisconsin, he had few clients. He ran unsuccessfully for district attorney but attracted the attention of a law firm in Shawano and was hired.

In 1938 Joe ran for Circuit Court judge. The incumbent was sixty-six, but McCarthy constantly described him as old and inefficient, and publicized the fact that the judge had earned

$200,000—not a huge amount considering his decades on the bench, which McCarthy never mentioned, but a sum that made Depression-era voters envious. McCarthy won the election and set about clearing up the backlog of cases the judge had allowed to pile up. Within months McCarthy had settled years' worth of litigation.

When World War II began, McCarthy realized that military service would be a political plus when he next ran for office. As a judge, he could have been exempted, but he took a leave of absence instead of resigning and enlisted in the Marine Corps. He later claimed he'd started out as a "buck private," the lowest rank, and risen to be an officer, but in fact he received a commission immediately, and instead of being put into combat, he was assigned to military intelligence. En route to Guadalcanal, during a party when the ship crossed the International Date Line, he slipped and broke some bones in his foot. He later claimed it was a "war wound," and when he campaigned, he walked with a limp and said he had "ten pounds of shrapnel" in his leg.

On Guadalcanal, he handled paperwork, not weapons. He wangled his way onto planes for several flights and later boasted that he'd flown an ever-increasing number of combat missions as "Tail-Gunner Joe."

A Wisconsin senator was running for reelection in 1944, and McCarthy decided to run against him, despite a law that forbade military officers from campaigning for public office. He got around that by taking a thirty-day leave, traveling around Wisconsin in his uniform and saying he was *not* campaigning, but *if* he were, this is what he'd say. He lost the election and returned to military duty but realized that no one had challenged his tales of combat. In the future, he would tell ever-bigger lies and seldom be forced to admit the truth.

McCarthy resigned his commission and returned to the bench, earning the reputation of turning his court into a "divorce mill," because of the speed with which he granted divorce decrees. He didn't care what people said about him, as long as his name was kept before the public. Having run earlier as a Democrat, he now changed parties, joining the Young Republicans where he saw more opportunity.

In 1946 Wisconsin's second senator, "Young Bob" La Follette, was up for reelection. The son of Progressive Robert La Follette, he'd served four terms in the U.S. Senate. In 1946 he left the Progressives for the Republicans, which pleased none of the three Wisconsin parties. The Progressives were angry at his departure, the Democrats thought he should have joined their party, and the Republicans wondered about his motives. McCarthy charged him, rightly, with neglecting Wisconsin in favor of national interests and defeated him in the primary.

Republican candidates all over America had an advantage that year. Americans were tired of war, the Depression, and the New Deal measures, all of which they connected to Democratic leaders. Republicans ran on the slogan, "Had enough? Time for a change." McCarthy won, becoming a U.S. senator at thirty-eight.

Not content to be just "one of the boys," McCarthy called a press conference to announce that he had a solution to the coal miners' strikes that were threatening the country. A few reporters showed up, curious about the brash newcomer. His idea was nothing new: Draft the miners into the army, order them to work, and shoot those who didn't for insubordination.

Frustrated at not being appointed to important committees, McCarthy took on sugar rationing as an issue. He wanted the rationing of sugar that began during the war ended so Wisconsin's sugar beet growers could increase production, and he was wooed with gifts and loans by the head of Pepsi-Cola, a big user of sugar. During the debate, he announced that there was plenty of sugar on hand and that the secretary of agriculture would allow each home canner twenty pounds. One senator slipped out, contacted the agriculture secretary and came back to expose McCarthy. Instead of admitting his subterfuge, McCarthy shouted that the other senator was lying. Rationing continued.

Public housing was his next issue. Private builders wined and dined McCarthy, and he dominated the committee that would recommend whether the government should subsidize public housing. At hearings across America, he arranged for those opposed to speak first and at length so that the pro–public housing speakers had little opportunity to express support. He slanted his report to show that most Americans opposed public housing. The bill failed to pass.

His next foray was into the Senate investigation of the Malmedy Massacre. In 1944 the Germans captured 150 American soldiers, marched them into a field outside the town of Malmedy, Belgium, and mowed them down with machine gun fire. Seventy-three perpetrators were captured and tried, and forty-three were sentenced to death. General Lucius Clay commuted the sentences of thirty-one men. The cases were reviewed by the War Crimes Board and the judge advocate and found to be sound. Then a Quaker group, the National Council for the Prevention of War, declared that the Germans had been tortured. An article appeared in several magazines under the byline of a pro-Fascist judge, Edward van Roden, claiming that the American prosecutors had committed heinous acts against the Malmedy perpetrators, kneeing them in the groin and kicking them. He later repudiated the statements, but it was too late. The furor swirled.

The secretary of the army stopped any executions of the remaining perpetrators, pending further investigation. The Senate decided to hold its own investigation. McCarthy was not on the investigative committee, but he was allowed to sit in on the hearings. He interrupted the proceedings rudely, attempted to confuse witnesses, and generally behaved despicably. He claimed the hearings were an attempt to "whitewash" the army. He got all the headlines, not the committee chairman, who soon resigned from the Senate. The army was cleared of any wrongdoing.

McCarthy was looking for some cause that would propel him to the forefront of the Senate, and he found it in Communism.

The time was ripe for a crusade against Communism. During the 1930s, some American intellectuals espoused the idea that the Soviet Union was the wave of the future, when property would be owned in common and everyone would be equal. Labor unions often had Communist members. Most Americans, however, viewed the events in Russia with horror, especially when word leaked out of mass starvation and political purges.

In the aftermath of World War II, the Soviet Union quickly took over Eastern Europe, Central Asia, and the Baltic states, and Communists attempted to overthrow the governments in Greece and Italy. Russia got the formula and materials for an atomic bomb, and Americans were frightened. China had a civil war, which ended with a Communist victory. Alger Hiss, a high-ranking State Department employee, was convicted of perjury in denying he had passed secrets to the Soviets. Then in June 1950, North Korea, which was under the influence of Russia, crossed the 38th Parallel and invaded South Korea. America was at war again.

Someone had to be responsible for the spread of Communism. But who? Americans wanted security, not the fear they might be blown up by an atomic bomb. Hysteria against Communism and Communist governments spread. The situation was ready-made for Joseph McCarthy.

His anti-Communist rants began on the evening of February 9, 1950, in Wheeling, West Virginia, where he was the speaker at the Lincoln Day dinner of the Ohio County Republican Women's Club. He spoke generally about the state of the country and then held up a list that he said contained the names of fifty-seven Communists employed by the State Department. His press release given to local newspapers and radio stations stated the number as 205. Over the next few days he spoke to other groups in cities across America, and the number varied. However, the number was not as newsworthy as the accusation itself. McCarthy was mobbed by the press at each stop and made headlines.

On February 20, he announced that he had acquired secret files of the State Department and read aloud in the Senate a lengthy list of a hundred names of employees suspected of being Communists or Communist sympathizers ("Comsymps" or "fellow travelers"). The list was not new; it had been compiled in 1947 and even included in the Congressional Record, but McCarthy had never taken note of it before. Of the hundred named, only forty-seven were employed by the State Department, and the FBI had cleared all of them. McCarthy criticized President Harry Truman for failing to release personnel files of other employees.

Why didn't his Senate colleagues challenge him? Democrats feared being called "soft on Communism," while Republicans thought this would show that they were "tough on Communism." McCarthy had also received many letters from voters saying they were glad someone was "doing something about the Communist threat," and he was becoming a star. A committee was appointed to investigate his charges. Its head was Millard Tydings of Maryland, whom McCarthy had tangled with during the Malmedy hearings.

McCarthy agreed to limit his list to the nine "most egregious" cases. He announced that he had uncovered the most dangerous Soviet spy in America but refused to state his name except to the committee behind closed doors. Naturally it was leaked to the press. The accused, Owen Lattimore, was not even employed by the government, but was a professor at Johns Hopkins University and a lecturer on the Far East. McCarthy could produce no evidence against Lattimore, and the committee issued a stinging rebuke of McCarthy.

In the election of 1950, McCarthy set out to defeat Tydings in revenge, raising money for his opponent and seeing to it that editorials criticized the incumbent as a "Comsymp." A political flyer included a doctored photo showing Tydings with Earl Browder, head of the Communist Party in America. It was a dirty trick, but it worked. Tydings lost, and others got the message: Don't oppose McCarthy.

Encouraged by his success at getting national attention, McCarthy attacked an American hero, General George C. Marshall. The general had commanded the American forces in World War II and had been secretary of state and secretary of defense. McCarthy was perhaps angry at Marshall, who admitted that he had counseled Truman to fire McCarthy's hero, General Douglas MacArthur, for insubordination. McCarthy accused Marshall of leading a conspiracy that turned China over to Communism. The speech was so long and so vitriolic that half of it was printed into the Congressional Record without McCarthy's reading it aloud, and it led even some of his supporters to question him. No evidence was ever found against the revered Marshall.

Still, McCarthy remained popular with voters, and 1952 was an election year. McCarthy accused the Democratic candidate for president, Adlai Stevenson, of meeting with a leading Communist, when in fact Stevenson had been in London on the day of the alleged meeting.

General Dwight "Ike" Eisenhower, the Republican presidential candidate, was persuaded to campaign in Wisconsin despite his dislike for McCarthy. Ike had written a speech that included a denunciation of McCarthy for his attacks on Marshall, but his advisers urged him to delete that portion. To Eisenhower's chagrin, McCarthy rushed forward after the speech and was photographed shaking Ike's hand.

In office now as part of the majority party, McCarthy was appointed to the Operations Committee for the District of Columbia, considered a "safe" place for him. However, he realized that the committee had a permanent Subcommittee for Investigations, and he took charge of the subcommittee, virtually ignoring the main committee. With his budget of $200,000, he hired staff and overshot himself, making several big mistakes.

FBI Director J. Edgar Hoover had cooperated with McCarthy, furnishing him information from FBI files, but even he began to back off from Tail-Gunner Joe. He warned McCarthy that he should thoroughly investigate his facts before making any further accusations. McCarthy ignored this advice and employed J. B. Matthews, who wrote an article claiming that the American Protestant church was the biggest supporter of Communism. This understandably infuriated American Protestants. McCarthy fired Matthews.

He next hired an FBI employee as his chief of staff. Hoover, realizing that any information McCarthy used would be directly connected to the FBI, severed ties with the senator.

McCarthy then hired his two most damaging employees, Roy Cohn and G. David Schine. Cohn was a brilliant young lawyer who had graduated from law school at nineteen. Schine, a wealthy playboy, had only one qualification: Cohn wanted him.

Throughout 1953, McCarthy and his team interrogated writers, artists, and musicians, accusing them of being Communists. Anyone who refused to answer or who took the Fifth Amendment against self-incrimination was deemed guilty. Those interrogated were asked to name their associates to protect themselves from further persecution, and the net spread.

That year McCarthy married his twenty-nine-year-old assistant, Jean Kerr. The wedding guests included members of Congress, the head of the CIA, and Vice President Richard Nixon. A congratulatory telegram arrived from the pope. McCarthy was at the peak of his popularity, but he was soon to fall.

Cohn urged McCarthy to investigate the CIA, but Ike put his foot down, and the idea was dropped.

Meanwhile, Cohn had evaded being drafted into the army, but Schine had been drafted and had failed to get a commission. Cohn tried to pull strings to get Schine a position with the CIA—though he had earlier urged a political attack on the agency—to keep him in Washington, but failed. Schine was sent to basic training in New Jersey. There he had privileges no other private enjoyed, including sixteen weekend or overnight passes in a three-month period and a car and driver to take him frequently to New York to rendezvous with Cohn. His basic training completed, Schine was assigned to a post in Georgia. Cohn went ballistic, making wild threats and vowing to wreck the army.

The excuse he used to destroy the military hierarchy was the promotion of a dentist who had admitted being a Communist and who was being discharged from the army. At Cohn's urging, McCarthy subpoenaed General Ralph Zwicker, commander of the post, demanding to know why he had promoted the dentist. McCarthy insulted the general, claiming he was "not fit to wear the uniform." Secretary of the Army Robert Stevens ordered Zwicker not to testify further, then met with McCarthy for what he had been told was to be a "conciliatory meeting." Instead, McCarthy told the press that Stevens had "surrendered" to him.

The tide was running against McCarthy. President Eisenhower issued a statement supporting Stevens, and Senator Ralph Flanders criticized McCarthy in the Senate. On January 25, 1954, CBS newscaster Edward R. Murrow broadcast a series of previously unseen clips of McCarthy speeches, the first of four programs. The viewing public was aghast at the senator's rudeness and arrogance.

Then the Pentagon released the record of the pressure Cohn had put on the army on behalf of Schine. McCarthy declared that instead the Army had put pressure on him. There would be hearings to determine the truth, and he demanded that the hearings be fully televised.

Of the three major networks, only ABC decided to carry the full hearings, which began on April 22, 1954. Joseph Welch was attorney for the army, while Cohn and McCarthy acted as their own lawyers. As the hearings went on for over a month, the audience grew, fascinated and repulsed at what they were seeing.

One of those who testified for the army mentioned in passing a meeting with the president. McCarthy immediately demanded the minutes of the meeting and subpoenaed those attending. Ike refused the demands. "Anyone who testifies about the advice he gave me won't be working for me that night," he said. He thwarted McCarthy, establishing "executive privilege," stating, "My people will not be subpoenaed."

Once again McCarthy was shown to have used a doctored photo, this one cropped to hint that Secretary Stevens was friendly with Schine, when Schine was actually part of a larger group and the secretary was smiling at someone who had been cropped out.

Welch's firm employed a young lawyer, Fred Fisher, who as a college student years before had belonged to the National Lawyers Guild, a Communist front organization. Fisher no longer belonged and was taking no part in the investigative hearings. McCarthy and Cohn had agreed beforehand not to bring this matter up if Welch did not mention Cohn's avoiding the draft.

However, at one point, Welch asked Cohn, "If you knew of Communists, would you turn them in?" McCarthy broke in to charge that Welch knowingly employed someone who continued to be a Communist and had not turned him in. He went on at length, accusing the young employee.

This was too much for Welch. The senator had persecuted the famous and powerful, but now he had broken his own agreement about Fisher, had knowingly accused him falsely, and in doing so would ruin the career of someone who was not present to defend himself. Moreover, it had nothing to do with the hearings, but was McCarthy's attempt to deflect attention away from their real purpose. Welch turned on McCarthy. "Until this moment, senator, I think I really never gauged your cruelty or your recklessness. Little did I dream that you could be so reckless and cruel as to do harm to that lad. . . . I fear he shall always bear a scar inflicted by you. If I could forgive you, I would, but I think your forgiveness must come from a higher place."

McCarthy broke in to complain that Welch had "baited" Cohn and attempted to say more about Fisher.

Welch stopped him. "I will not discuss this further with you, senator. Have you no sense of decency, sir, at long last?"

There was applause from the gallery, and as Welch walked out, McCarthy sat slumped in his chair, unapologetic.

McCarthy's fellow senators censured him, not for his lies and damaged lives, but for his behavior in the Senate and in disobeying a summons from a committee. It was a very watered-down censure, and if he had apologized, he might have avoided even that.

But his power was broken. Americans had seen him for the bully he was and felt only revulsion for him.

Always a heavy drinker, he sank into alcoholism and died on May 2, 1957, of cirrhosis of the liver.

Despite his "crusade," McCarthy's attack on Communism failed to produce a single known subversive or a single conviction for treason or any other act against the American government. The real anti-Communist work had already been done by the House Un-American Activities Committee, and the Communist Party USA was even then a weak organization. "Tail-Gunner Joe" had spent his talent and influence on an evil enterprise, attacking others to get attention for himself. His name is forever linked to a dark period in American history. Knowingly attacking the character of innocent people is called "McCarthyism."

Sources

The prolific writer of history and current events, Robert Goldston, wrote one of the first McCarthy biographies, *The American Nightmare: Senator Joseph R. McCarthy and the Politics of Hate* (Indianapolis, Ind.: Bobbs-Merrill, 1973). Tom Wicker's *Shooting Star: The Brief Arc of Joe McCarthy* (New York: Harcourt, 2006) presents more background, since it was published after the Venona Project—*Venona: Decoding Soviet Espionage in America* (New Haven, Conn.: Yale University Press, 1999). The release of this information showed that in many ways America's fears of Communism were not misplaced and revealed that Alger Hiss *had* been guilty. *Joe McCarthy and the Press* by Edwin R. Bayley (Madison: University of Wisconsin Press, 1981) details how McCarthy used the press to further his career and how the press used him.

Two other books I consulted each have a chapter on McCarthy: Lawrance Binda's *The Big Bad Book of Republicans* (Washington, D.C.: Pazzo Press, 2005) has a chapter entitled, "Joseph McCarthy—Washington Witch Hunt." In *A Treasury of Great American Scandals* by Michael Farquhar (New York: Penguin Books, 2003), McCarthy is depicted as "Wisconsin Sleaze."

Bibliography

BOOKS

Ackerman, Kenneth D. *Young J. Edgar: Hoover, the Red Scare and the Assault on Civil Liberties*. New York: Carroll & Graf Publishers, 2007.

Adams, John. *John Adams, A Biography in His Own Words*. Edited by James Bishop Peabody. New York: Newsweek Publishers, 1973.

Anthony, Carl Sferrazza. *Florence Harding: The First Lady, the Jazz Age and the Death of America's Most Scandalous President*. New York: William Morrow, 1998.

Bagley, Edwin R. *Joe McCarthy and the Press*. Madison: University of Wisconsin Press, 1981.

Beveridge, Albert J. *The Life of John Marshall, Vol. III: Conflict and Construction*. Boston: Houghton Mifflin, 1919.

Binda, Lawrance. *The Big Bad Book of Democrats*. Washington, D.C.: Pazzo Press, 2005.

———. *The Big Bad Book of Republicans*. Washington, D.C.: Pazzo Press, 2005.

Bishop, Jim. *The Day Lincoln Was Shot*. New York: Bantam Books, 1953.

Brandt, Nat. *The Congressman Who Got Away With Murder*. Syracuse, N.Y.: Syracuse University Press, 1991.

Bruns, Roger. *Thomas Jefferson*. New York: Chelsea House Publishers, 1986.

Burr, Samuel Engle, Jr. *Colonel Aaron Burr, the American Phoenix*. New York: Exposition Press, 1961.

Burstein, Andrew. *The Passions of Andrew Jackson.* New York: Alfred A. Knopf, 2003.

Campbell, Tom W. *Two Fighters and Two Fines: Sketches of the Lives of Matthew Lyon and Andrew Jackson.* Little Rock, Ark.: Pioneer Publishing Company, 1941.

Clarfield, Gerard. *Timothy Pickering and American Diplomacy 1795–1800.* Columbia: University of Missouri Press, 1969.

———. *Timothy Pickering and the American Republic.* Pittsburgh, Pa.: University of Pittsburgh Press, 1980.

Cunliffe, Marcus. *The Nation Takes Shape 1789–1837.* Chicago: University of Chicago Press, 1959.

Dead Last: The Public Memory of Warren G. Harding's Scandalous Legacy. Athens: Ohio University Press, 2009 (various contributors).

Dean, John W. *Warren G. Harding.* New York: Henry Holt, 2004.

De Angelis, Gina. *It Happened in Washington, D.C.* Guilford, Conn.: Globe Pequot Press, 2004.

Demaris, Ovid. *The Director: An Oral History of J. Edgar Hoover.* New York: Harper's Magazine Press, 1975.

Donald, David. *Charles Sumner and the Coming of the Civil War.* New York: Alfred A. Knopf, 1960.

Dunning, William Archibald. *Reconstruction—Political and Economic.* New York: Harper & Brothers, 1907.

Ehle, John. *Trail of Tears: The Rise and Fall of the Cherokee Nation.* New York: Random House, 1988.

Ellis, Joseph L. *American Sphinx: The Character of Thomas Jefferson.* New York: Alfred A. Knopf, 1997.

Farquhar, Michael. *A Treasury of Great American Scandals.* New York: Penguin Books, 2003.

Finan, Christopher M. *From the Palmer Raids to the Patriot Act: A History of the Fight for Free Speech in America*. Boston: Beacon Press, 2007.

Fleming, Thomas J. *Thomas Jefferson*. New York: Grosset & Dunlap, 1969.

Franklin, John Hope. *Reconstruction: After the Civil War*. Chicago: University of Chicago Press, 1961.

Gentry, Curt. *J. Edgar Hoover—The Man and the Secrets*. New York: W.W. Norton, 1991.

Giblin, James Cross. *Good Brother, Bad Brother*. New York: Clarion Books, 2005.

Goldston, Robert. *The American Nightmare: Senator Joseph R. McCarthy and the Politics of Hate*. Indianapolis, Ind.: Bobbs Merrill, 1973.

Goodrich, Thomas. *The Darkest Dawn: Lincoln, Booth, and the Great American Tragedy*. Bloomington: Indiana University Press, 2005.

Haw, James, and Francis F. Bierne, Rosamond P. Bierne and R. Samuel Jett. *Stormy Patriot—The Life of Samuel Chase*. Baltimore: Maryland Historical Society, 1980.

Hendrickson, Robert A. *Hamilton II 1789–1804*. New York: Mason/Charter Books, 1976.

———. *The Rise and Fall of Alexander Hamilton*. New York: Van Nostrand Reinhold Company, 1981.

Hoogenboom, Ari. *Rutherford B. Hayes, Warrior and President*. Lawrence: University of Kansas Press, 1995.

Kauffman, Michael W. *American Brutus*. New York: Random House, 2004.

Kaufman, Bill. *Forgotten Founder, Drunken Prophet: The Life of Luther Martin.* Wilmington, Del.: ISI Books, 2008.

Keneally, Thomas. *American Scoundrel: The Life of the Notorious Civil War General Dan Sickles.* New York: Doubleday, 2002.

Kennedy, Roger G. *Burr, Hamilton and Jefferson.* New York: Oxford University Press, 2000.

Kessler, Ronald. *Inside Congress.* New York: Pocket Books, 1997.

———. *The Bureau: The Secret History of the FBI.* New York: St. Martin's Paperbacks, 2002.

Klein, Philip Shriver. *President James Buchanan.* University Park: The Pennsylvania State University Press, 1962.

Knappman, Edward W., ed. *American Trials of the 20th Century.* Detroit: Visible Ink Press, 1994.

Larson, Edward J. *A Magnificent Catastrophe: The Tumultuous Election of 1800.* New York: Simon & Schuster, 2007.

Lexington, Fayette (pseudonym). *The Celebrated Case of Colonel W. C. P. Breckinridge and Madeline Pollard.* Chicago: The Current Events Publishing Company, 1894.

Lomask, Milton. *Aaron Burr, the Years from Princeton to Vice President, 1756–1805.* New York: Farrar, Strauss & Giroux, 1979.

Long, Kim. *The Almanac of Political Corruption, Scandals and Dirty Politics.* New York: Random House, 2007.

Longacre, Edward G. *General Ulysses S. Grant, the Soldier and the Man.* Cambridge, Mass.: Da Capo Press, 2007.

Malone, Dumas. *Jefferson and His Time, Volume 4, Jefferson the President, First Term 1801–1805.* New York: Little, Brown and Company, 1970.

McCartney, Laton. *The Teapot Dome Scandal.* New York: Random House, 2009.

Melton, Buckner F. *Aaron Burr: Conspiracy to Treason*. New York: John Wiley & Sons, 2001.

Miller, John C. *Crisis in Freedom: The Alien and Sedition Acts*. Boston: Little, Brown and Company, 1951.

Morris, Roy Jr. *Fraud of the Century: Rutherford B. Hayes, Samuel Tilden and the Stolen Election of 1876*. New York: Simon & Schuster, 2003.

Murray, Robert K. *The Harding Era*. Minneapolis: The University of Minnesota Press, 1969.

Napolitano, Judge Andrew. *Dred Scott's Revenge*. Nashville, Tenn.: Thomas Nelson Co., 2009.

Nevins, Allen. *Ordeal of the Union: A House Divided, 1852–1857*. New York: Charles Scribner's Sons, 1947.

Perret, Geoffrey. *Ulysses S. Grant—Soldier & President*. New York: The Modern Library, 1997.

Rehnquist, William H. *Centennial Crisis: The Disputed Election of 1876*. New York: Random House, 2004.

_____. *Grand Inquests: The Historic Impeachments of Justice Samuel Chase and President Andrew Johnson*. New York: William Morrow, 1992.

Remini, Robert V. *Andrew Jackson and His Indian Wars*. New York: Viking, 2001.

———. *The Life of Andrew Jackson*. New York, Harper & Row, 1988.

———. *The Revolutionary Age of Andrew Jackson*. New York, Harper & Row, 1976.

Ross, Shelley. *Fall from Grace: Sex, Scandal and Corruption in American Politics from 1702 to the Present*. New York: Random House, 1988.

Russell, Francis. *The Shadow of Blooming Grove: Warren G. Harding in His Times.* New York: McGraw-Hill, 1968.

Severn, Bill. *John Marshall, the Man Who Made the Court Supreme.* New York: David McKay Co., 1969.

Simon, James L. *Lincoln and Chief Justice Taney.* New York: Simon & Schuster, 2006.

Sloan, Cliff, and David McKean. *The Great Decision—Jefferson, Adams, Marshall and the Battle for the Supreme Court.* New York: Perseus Books, 2009.

Smelser, Marshall. *The Democratic Republic 1801–1815.* New York: Harper & Row Publishers, 1968.

Stampp, Kenneth M. *The Era of Reconstruction 1865–1877.* New York: Alfred A. Knopf, 1976.

Steers, Edward Jr. *Blood on the Moon.* Lexington: University of Kentucky Press, 2001.

Stern, Philip Van Doren. *The Man Who Killed Lincoln: The Story of John Wilkes Booth and His Part in the Assassination.* New York: Literary Guild, 1939.

Stone, Geoffrey R. *Perilous Times: Free Speech in Wartime from the Sedition Act of 1798 to the War on Terrorism.* New York: W.W. Norton, 2004.

Summers, Anthony. *Official and Confidential: The Secret Life of J. Edgar Hoover.* New York: G.P. Putnam, 1993.

Swanberg, W. A. *Sickles the Incredible.* Gettysburg, Pa.: Stan Clark Military Books, 1956.

Swisher, Carl Brent. *Roger B. Taney.* New York: Macmillan Company, 1935.

Vidal, Gore. *Inventing a Nation.* New Haven, Conn.: Yale University Press, 2003.

Weisner, Herman B. *The Politics of Justice: A. B. Fall and the Teapot Dome Scandal.* Albuquerque, N.M.: Creative Designs, 1988.

Weymouth, Lally. *America in 1876: The Way We Were.* New York: Random House, 1976.

Wheelan, Joseph. *Jefferson's Vendetta.* New York: Carroll & Graf Publishers, 2005.

White, Leonard D. *The Federalists.* New York: Macmillan Company, 1956.

Wicker, Tom. *Shooting Star: The Brief Arc of Joe McCarthy.* New York: Harcourt Inc., 2006.

MAGAZINES AND NEWSPAPERS

Anglo-American Times (London). "Running for Governor of Massachusetts." September 14, 1872, p. 10.

Atlanta Constitution. "A Girl Spy's Story—Spied on Pollard During Trial." June 24, 1894, p. 9.

Bear, James A. Jr. "The Hemings Family at Monticello." *Virginia Cavalcade,* Vol. XXIX, Autumn 1979, p. 78.

Chester (Pa.) Times. "Suppress Russian Workers Aim of Red Raids," November 9, 1919, p. 1.

Dabney, Virginius, and Jon Kukla. "The Monticello Scandals." *Virginia Cavalcade,* Vol. XXIX, Autumn 1979, p. 72.

Decatur (Ill.) Daily Republican. "A Man's Perfidy." March 21, 1894, p. 2.

(Indianapolis) Indiana Progress. "The Nation Mourns." March 18, 1874, p. 4.

Jellison, Charles A. "James Thomson Callender." *Virginia Cavalcade*, Vol. XXIX, Autumn 1979, p. 62.

Langhorne, Elizabeth. "Edward Coles, Thomas Jefferson, and the Rights of Man." *Virginia Cavalcade*, Vol. XXIII, Summer 1973, p. 30.

Lowell (Mass.) Sun. "Got $15,000." April 16, 1894, p. 6.

———. "Nationwide Roundup." November 10, 1919, p. 1.

Marion (Ohio) Daily Star. "Reds Bomb Homes and Start Reign of Terror." June 3, 1919, p. 1.

New Castle (Pa.) News. "Letters to Rhodes." March 28, 1894, p. 8.

New York Times. "Miss Pollard Disparaged." March 29, 1894, p. 2.

———. Obituary of W. C. P. Breckinridge. November 18, 1904, p. 1.

Royster, Charles. "A Battle of Memoirs: Lighthorse Harry Lee and Thomas Jefferson." *Virginia Cavalcade,* Vol. XXXI, Autumn 1981, p. 112.

Steubenville (Ohio) Weekly Herald. "Raids on Alleged Plotters Against the Government." November 13, 1919, p.3.

———. "Nets Are Laid to Nab Reds." November 13, 1919, p.10.

Tyrone (Pa.) Daily Herald. "Bombs Planted in Many Cities." June 4, 1919, p. 1.

WEB SITES

"A Complete and Graphic Account of the Crédit Mobilier Investigation." Central Pacific Railroad Photographic History Museum Web site. http://cprr.org/Museum/Credit_Mobilier_1873.html (accessed April 2, 2010).

"Albert B. Fall." Wikipedia. http://en.wikipedia.org/wiki/Albert_B._Fall (accessed March 2, 2010).

"Alexander Mitchell Palmer." Wikipedia. http://en.wikipedia.org/wiki/Alexander_Mitchell_Palmer (accessed March 2, 2010).

"A. Mitchell Palmer." NNDB. www.nndb.com/people/233/000166732/ (accessed March 2, 2010).

Baker, Kevin. "When Mudslinging in Congress Led to Actual Bloodshed." www.kevinbaker.info/c_cp (accessed December 19, 2009).

"Chase, Samuel (1741–1811)." Maryland Online Encyclopedia. www.mdoe.org/chasesamuel.html (accessed December 20, 2010).

"Dred Scott v. Sandford." Wikipedia. http://en.wikipedia.org/wiki/Dred_scott_v._sandford (accessed January 15, 2010).

www.fbi.gov/page2/dec07/palmerraids122807.html (accessed March 2, 2010).

"General Sickles Visits His Troops." History.com. www.history.com/this-day-in-history/general-sickles-visits-his-troops (accessed December 2, 2009).

www.Rogerjnorton.com/Lincoln72.html (accessed January 9, 2010).

"Impeachment Trial of Samuel Chase." Answers.com. www.answers.com/topic/impeachment-trial-of-samuel-chase (accessed Nov. 3, 2009).

"James T. Callender." Wikipedia. http://en.wikipedia.org/wiki /James_T._Callender (accessed December 31, 2009).

"John Fries Rebellion Part 2: The Trial." www.jamesmannartfarm .com/friesreb2.html (accessed December 20, 2009).

"Orville E. Babcock." Wikipedia. http://en.wikipedia.org/wiki /Orville_E._Babcock (accessed March 28, 2010).

"Roger Taney." Wikipedia. http://en.wikipedia.org/wiki/Roger_ Taney (accessed December 19, 2009).

"Samuel Chase." Wikipedia. http://en.wikipedia.org/wiki/Samuel_ Chase (accessed November 3, 2009).

www.senate.gov/artandhistory/history/minute/War_Secretarys_ Impeachment_Trial.htm (accessed April 2, 2010).

Shenkman, Rick. "The Last High White House Official Indicted While in Office: U.S. Grant's Orville Babcock." History News Network, October 31, 2005. http://hnn.us/articles/17562.html (accessed April 2, 2010).

"Timothy Pickering." Wikipedia. http://en.wikipedia.org/wiki /Timothy_Pickering (accessed January 11, 2010).

"Volusian Confusion: Tilden-Hayes." History House, November 20, 2000. www.historyhouse.com/uts/tilden_hayes/ (accessed March 22, 2010).

"Whiskey Ring." Wikipedia. http://en.wikipedia.org/wiki/Whiskey _Ring (accessed March 28, 2010).

"William Breckinridge Breach of Promise Trial: 1894—A Relationship Blossoms." http://law.jrank.org/pages2709/William-Breckinridge-Breach-Promise-Trial-1894 (accessed November 19, 2009).

"William W. Belknap." Wikipedia. http://en.wikipedia.org/wiki /William_W._Belknap (accessed April 2, 2010).

Index

About the Author

Emilee Hines, a native Virginian, is the author of four previous books for Globe Pequot Press: *It Happened in Virginia, More Than Petticoats: Remarkable Virginia Women, Mysteries and Legends of Virginia,* and *Virginia: Mapping the Old Dominion State through History.* She lives in Hendersonville, North Carolina.